Beginning Neo4j

Chris Kemper

Apress®

Beginning Neo4j

ISBN-13 (pbk): 978-1-4842-1228-8

ISBN-13 (electronic): 978-1-4842-1227-1

Managing Director: Welmoed Spahr
Lead Editor: Louise Corrigan
Technical Reviewer: Sam Stites
Editorial Board: Steve Anglin, Pramila Balen, Louise Corrigan, Jim DeWolf, Jonathan Gennick, Robert Hutchinson, Celestin Suresh John, Michelle Lowman, James Markham, Susan McDermott, Matthew Moodie, Jeffrey Pepper, Douglas Pundick, Ben Renow-Clarke, Gwenan Spearing
Coordinating Editor: Melissa Maldonado
Copy Editor: Lori Cavanaugh
Compositor: SPi Global
Indexer: SPi Global
Artist: SPi Global

Distributed to the book trade worldwide by Springer Science+Business Media New York, 233 Spring Street, 6th Floor, New York, NY 10013. Phone 1-800-SPRINGER, fax (201) 348-4505, e-mail orders-ny@springer-sbm.com, or visit www.springer.com. Apress Media, LLC is a California LLC and the sole member (owner) is Springer Science + Business Media Finance Inc (SSBM Finance Inc). SSBM Finance Inc is a Delaware corporation.

For information on translations, please e-mail rights@apress.com, or visit www.apress.com.

Apress and friends of ED books may be purchased in bulk for academic, corporate, or promotional use. eBook versions and licenses are also available for most titles. For more information, reference our Special Bulk Sales–eBook Licensing web page at www.apress.com/bulk-sales.

Any source code or other supplementary material referenced by the author in this text is available to readers at www.apress.com. For detailed information about how to locate your book's source code, go to www.apress.com/source-code/.

To my friends, family, and caffeine.

Contents at a Glance

Contents

About the Author

Chris Kemper was born and bred in the North of England. Growing up, he spent his time taking computers apart and putting them back together. So with such a clever mind, it's no surprise he got into web development in his early teens.

Since graduating in 2008, Chris has expanded his knowledge of web development by working for some big names within the North East, honing his development skills, and keeping up with modern trends.

Chris is always at the cutting-edge of his field, which often means he has lots of big ideas but frustratingly, not enough time to bring them to fruition.

Already a published author, he loves to share his expertise and relishes in discussing tech problems and solutions. What's most impressive is his ability to articulate such a difficult subject into words and more so, do it in such a way that it's easy to understand.

You can catch Chris on Twitter at @ChrisDKemper, or check out his personal site http://chrisdkemper.co.uk.

About the Technical Reviewer

Sam Stites is a functional, polyglot engineer coming from a background in statistics and data science.

Acknowledgments

Throughout this process I've had help, support, and encouragement from so many different people, It'd be a long list to name them all. Whether it was with support, or just telling me to get myself in gear, I couldn't have done this without you all.

I owe a special thanks to Mr. Sherry, who as always has kept me on the right path with support and advice, sprinkled with colorful (scouse) language. I'd also like to take this chance to thank Mr. Sterling, and Mr. Wardle, because I know without those two, I'd not be in the position I am today.

I have to give a big thanks to my family for putting up with my distance during the project, and giving me nothing but support for the duration. To try and make it up to people in my own way, you'll see various names in code examples throughout the book. I may not have been with my family or friends, but at least I could include them, even if it's just in examples.

Whether it was just letting me vent, allowing me to bounce ideas off you, or even giving me advice, I know many people have helped me in more ways than I can acknowledge, thank you. Finally, I'd like to thank everybody that helped me with the website I created for the book (see Chapter 7 for that). Whether you just shared it on Twitter or Facebook, or if you actually submitted your data, I'd like to thank you all for doing so.

Introduction

Whether we like it or not, the world is becoming more connected, and at some point in the very near future, your toaster may well be able to recommend types of bread. The information could be recommended products from retailers or suggested friends on Social Networks; whatever it is, you'll be able to see the benefits (if you like the recommendations, that is) of using graph databases. This book will take you right through from knowing nothing about graphs and graph databases or Neo4j, to knowing how to write your own recommendation system, using language that's easy to understand.

It aims to cover the theory early on, and get to the practical (in this case, coding) side of Neo4j, in the form of Cypher, Neo4j's query language. You'll learn what Cypher actually is in Chapter 4, and also how to use it to interact with your data as the book progresses. And Chapter 7 is where things start to get interesting.

Speaking of data, Beginning Neo4j will also contain a number of data examples to help model your data, or be used as a reference for your own projects. After you've installed Neo4j on your system (covered in Chapter 3) you'll then be taken through the process of how to host your Neo4j application online.

A big issue with books that reference code is that by their very nature, over time things inevitably change, and code may not work as it once did in future versions. To avoid this, in certain instances, code will be hosted online and it'll be explained as and when it's needed during the course of the book.

In addition, there will be a micro site available at `http://chrisdkemper.co.uk/beginning-neo4j` that will contain links to the items mentioned in the various chapters. I'll aim to keep this website and the content it contains as up to date as possible, so check there for updates. If you do happen to notice something that's now incorrect, or missing, please try to get in touch with me and I'll do my best to fulfil your request.

Contacting Chris Kemper

The easiest way to get in touch will be via e-mail at `hey@chrisdkemper.co.uk`. If you'd prefer to take the social media approach, it's `@ChrisDKemper` on Twitter. All being well, I'll try my best to help out and answer any questions.

CHAPTER 1

■ ■ ■

Introduction to Graph Databases

With anything that's worth learning, there's always a bit of theory to go along with something more practical, and this book is no exception. Neo4j is the leading graph database (or at least that's how they describe themselves, anyway), but what does that mean? If you're from a more traditional relational-database approach, then the concept of a graph database may be a new one, but learning a bit of theory will be worth it. Graph databases have many advantages, one of which is making some queries that are close to impossible in traditional SQL based databases, very possible using a graph database. Graph databases make this possible because their primary function is to relate data. If you understand graph databases already, you could skip ahead, but my teachers always used to say: "Well it's a good refresher for you," so I'll say the same, and hopefully there's a benefit.

In this chapter, I'll be covering everything database related to show why graph databases are a brilliant utility, and how they have a lot of potential for modern application development. There's already a number of people, from large companies, such as eBay and WalMart, to small research teams taking advantage of graph databases to solve various data-based problems, and you could be too. Of course there are many databases out there. Where do graph databases stand? This chapter will also give an overview on the various types of databases and a few details on each one.

What is a database?

Before going into detail about graph databases, relational-databases, or any database for that matter, it's probably a good idea to start at the beginning, and describing what a database actually is. At its most fundamental, a database is primarily a means of organizing information. Databases come in many forms. Most are associated with the computer system but some are used for backups.

Since a database is a structured set of information, it doesn't need to be limited to something electronic. A hard copy address book and an electronic address book are both structured data and are both considered databases. However, there may be a time when you want to migrate to a more reliable database system that isn't paper based. When you do, you need to know where to start. To manage data in a traditional database and communicate with your chosen database, you'll use a Database management system (DBMS). There are many DBMSs on the market, such as MySQL, PostgreSQL, Microsoft SQL Server, CouchDB, or (Of course) Neo4j. If you aren't familiar with any of those, or your particular favorite wasn't mentioned don't worry. There are a lot of different DBMSs on the market, each with its own advantages and disadvantages, depending on your use case.

A database system allows you to interact with the data stored within it via a predetermined language, dictated by the type of database. The main job of a DBMS is to provide a way for the user to interact with the data stored in it. These interactions can be categorized into four primary sections:

- **Data definition** – Any action that modifies the organization of the data within the database

- **Update** - When an action manipulates the actual data stored within the databases is classed as an update, which includes creating, updating, and deleting data. In the case of inserting or deleting data, this is classed as an update to the database itself as you're changing the data structure in some way by either adding or removing data.

- **Retrieval** - Data is stored in a database in most cases to be reused. When data is selected from the database to be used in another application, that's a retrieval.

- **Administration** – The remaining actions of user management, performance analysis, security, and all of the higher-level actions are classes as administration.

Database Transactions

Depending on your knowledge of databases the idea of transactions may be a new concept. It's one of those things you may know about, but not know the correct words to explain it. A database transaction is essentially a group of queries that all have to be successful for them to be applied. If one query within a transaction fails, the whole thing does. Database transactions have two main purposes, both involving consistency, just in different ways.

The first purpose of a database transaction is to ensure that all queries within a transaction are actually executed, which can be very important. Say you're creating a user and inserting a record for it into the database. There are cases when the ID of an inserted row will be used in queries that follow it. One use is permissions or roles, where a user's id would traditionally be used to make the relation. If that initial creation of the user fails, maybe due to not being unique, the subsequent queries will also fail since they depend on the result of the failed query. Depending on how the application is set up, if these queries were run without using the transaction incomplete data may be added to the database (so potentially a set of permissions for a non-existent user) or for the application to fail unexpectedly. To avoid this, you can run all of the queries within a transaction, so if any query fails, then any queries that have already run (within the transaction) are reverted, and the query ends, which means your data is untouched.

The second purpose of a database transaction concerns two actions happening at the same time: if a database is being queried simultaneously by multiple sources, then there is the potential the data integrity may be compromised. For example, if you were querying the database, but also performing an update on some of the data being queried at the same time, what would happen? To make this example more informative, let's say we're querying a list of users by name, but one of the users is online changing their name. Depending on the timing of the query (without transactions) there's a chance you could get the data before or even after the change; there isn't any guarantee. Using transactions though, the update would only be committed and then available to query after it and all other queries within said transaction were successful. So in this case, the updated name wouldn't be available until all of the needed queries within the transaction were successful.

When you talk about a database transaction, it should be atomic, consistent, isolated, and durable, or ACID. If a database transaction is truly ACID, then it works as it's been explained here, in an all-or-nothing fashion. The most important time for a transaction to abide by the ACID principles is when money is involved. For instance, if you had a system in place to pay bills, which transferred money from one account to another, and then made a payment, you'd want to ensure all of that happened without any errors. If the bills account was empty, the money transfer from one account to the other would fail, but if the two actions were run outside of a single transaction, you would still try to make the payment, even though no money had been transferred. This is an example of when a query is executed, then subsequent queries depend on the result of the first one, and in this case, you'd want both queries to be in one, ACID-compliant transaction.

Principles used within ACID are relative to the CAP Theorem, also known as Brewer's Theorem. Eric Brewer (the theorem's creator) stated that it is impossible for a distributed computer system (or database) to simultaneously guarantee the following three conditions:

- Consistency (data is available to all nodes at the same time)

- Availability (each request receives a response about whether it was successful or failed)

- Partition tolerance (the system can still operate despite losing contact with other nodes due to network issues)

If a system of nodes (or databases) wants to be always available, and safe from failures, then it cannot always have the most up-to-date data. For example, if you have a system of three nodes, each node would be a copy of the last, so if one failed, you would have access to the other two. If you were to make a change to one of the nodes, then the other two nodes would be unaware of the change. To combat this problem, Eventual Consistency is implied, meaning that through some means, eventually, the change would be mirrored across all three nodes. In relation to ACID, until a transaction has completed, the contents of that transaction won't be available to access within a database. Essentially, CAP, is ACID, but applied to a distributed system.

Many database vendors rave about their software being fully ACID compliant, so this was just a quick overview to show what that actually is. Although a lot of different systems support ACID, it's not something that just happens. In most cases you'll need to show you want to start a transaction, which can be different depending on the query language used, but the concept is the same. Once the transaction has been initialized, the queries running within it are added. Then when it needs to be committed, this is added to the query in the way the language requires it. There are cases when you simply don't need transactions, so just remember when you want to use a transaction, you'll probably have to indicate it in the query, unless your chosen database vendor has different rules.

Although transactions are used with the intention of rolling them back if they fail, this isn't always the desired outcome. In some cases, such as in MySQL, you need to explicitly say if you want to rollback a failed transaction, and this can only be done before the transaction is committed. Each database vendor will have its own rules when it comes to how transactions are handled, so if you want to use them just be sure to check the official documentation to ensure you're using them correctly.

What is a Graph?

Trying to define what a graph actually is isn't the easiest of tasks, as it has a variety of meanings depending on the context. In a traditional sense, graphs are used to display how two or more systems of data relate to each other. A basic example could be something as simple as, number of pies eaten over a certain time period, or pies over time. The graph seen in Figure 1-1 illustrates that very example, and shows a way of representing pies over time.

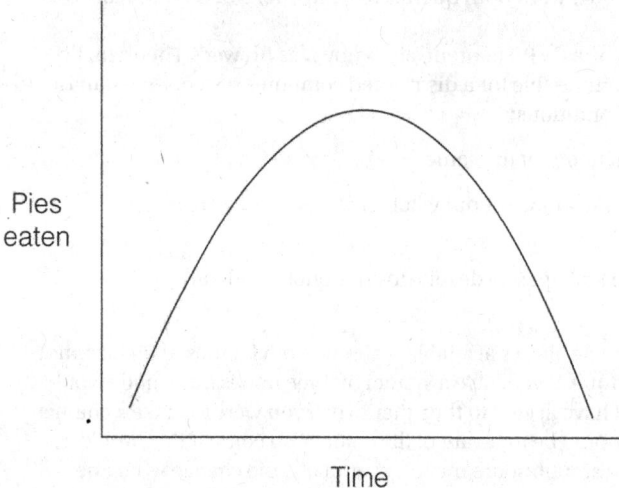

Figure 1-1. *A basic graph showing how pies are eaten over time*

If you were grading this graph it would be very a low one, there aren't any units on the axis and the origin hasn't been marked with a value. Although it's not the most imperative graph, it does still show (assuming the units would increase from the graph origin) that as time goes on, more pies are eaten, then after so long, the rate in which pies are eaten goes down. Graphs of this nature are normally called a bell curve, or an inverted U, depending on the context, where a graph hits a maximum point, and curves on either side, causing a bell shape.

The example used here was a graph showing pies over time, but there are of course many, many more graphs and graph types out there. Graphs can range from the serious (Showing important data, company growth), to the not so serious (I'm sure we've all seen some crude ones) but no matter the subject matter, the graphs all share one common trend, a relationship. In our example the relationship is pies with time, but you could equally have something like profits and time in a graph showing company growth. Getting this relationship is the key part of what makes a graph a graph, and applying that to a mathematics-based graph or to a graph database is the same concept.

When it comes to the mathematical graphs, you can have the different data systems relating using various different graph types, such as a line graph, bar chart, or even a pie chart. Some very literal examples of these can be seen in Figure 1-2.

In graph databases, you wouldn't necessarily see the data shown in any of those formats, although given that graph nodes are represented by a relationship, they are still graphs. Regardless of the complexity of the graph, even if it's just a small, simple one, it can be translated to a graph database, to allow it to be queried and analyzed.

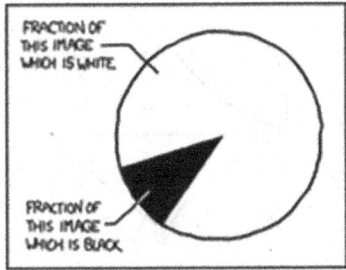 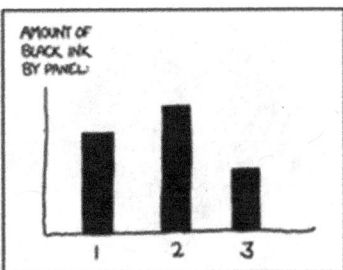 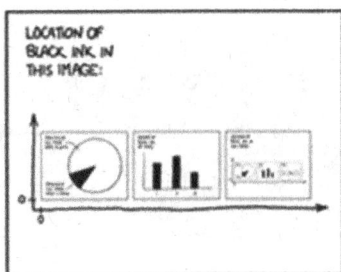

Figure 1-2. A comic from xkcd 688 showing some very literal, self-describing graphs

Graph Theory

If you were to simplify graph theory, you could say it was just that, the study of graphs, but there is a lot more to it than that. Developers have been taking the principles of graph theory and applying them to databases. Thanks to this hard work there are graph databases, that take relating data very seriously.

In a mathematical sense, graph theory is the study of structures used to model the relationship between objects. In this context, a graph is made up of *nodes* (or *vertices*) and potentially *edges* connecting them. If you wanted to demonstrate this visually, it can be done with an arrow to indicate that a node is connected to another node. For example, if we had two nodes, A and B, to which A was connected to B with an edge, it could be expressed as A ➤ B. The direction is shown here in that A is connected to B, but B is not connected to A. If the edges that make up a graph don't have an associated direction (e.g., A ➤ B is the same as B ➤ A), then the graph is classed as *undirected*. If however, the orientation of the edge has some meaning, then the graph is *directed*.

There are other applications for graph theory outside the world of mathematics. Since graph theory, at its lowest level, describes how data relates to each other, it can be applied to a number of different industries and scenarios where relating data is important. It can be used to map out chemical structures, create road diagrams, even to analyze data from social networks. The applications for graph theory are pretty wide.

Origins

The first known paper on graph theory was written way back in 1736 called "Seven Bridges of Königsberg" by Leonhard Euler, a brilliant mathematician and physicist, considered to be the pre-eminent mathematician of the 18th century. He introduced a lot of the notation and terminology used within modern mathematics, and published extensively within the fields of fluid dynamics, astronomy, and even music theory. Leonhard Euler was an incredible man and helped further modern mathematics and other fields to where they are today. If you have a chance to read up on him. Right now though, we will focus on "Seven Bridges of Königsberg," from which graph theory originated.

The city of Königsberg, Prussia (now Kaliningrad, Russia) was built on top of the Pregel River, and included two large islands that were connected to each other and the mainland by seven bridges. The problem was to see if it were possible to cross each of Königsberg's seven bridges just once, and be able to visit all the parts of the city. You can see an abstracted version of the problem in Figure 1-3.

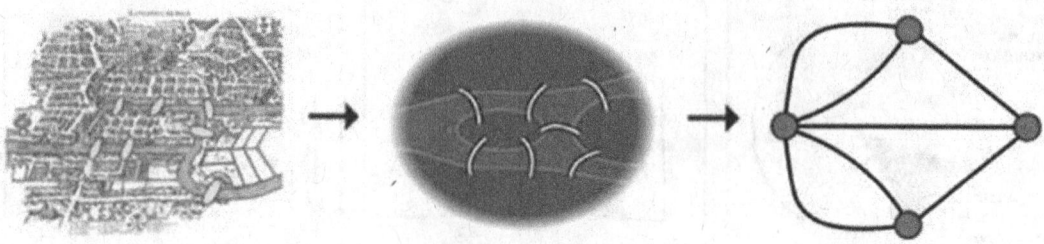

Figure 1-3. *The 7 bridges of Königsberg, abstracted into a graph format*

After abstracting the problem into a graph, Euler noticed a pattern, based on the number of vertices and edges. In the Königsberg graph, there are 4 vertices and 7 edges. In the literal sense, Euler noticed that if you were to walk to one of the islands, and exit to another, you would use an entrance bridge, and an exit bridge. Essentially, to be able to traverse a path across a graph without crossing an edge more than once, you need an *even* number of edges.

Euler theorized that to traverse a graph entirely, by using each edge only once, depends on a node's degrees. In the context of a node or vertex, degrees refers to the amount of edges touching the node. Euler argued that if you were to traverse a graph fully (using an edge only once), you can have either 0, or 2 nodes of odd degrees. This was later proven by Carl Hierholzer, and traversing a graph in this way is known as an Eulerian path or Euler walk in Euler's honor.

Graph Databases

Using graph theory as a basis, graph databases store data in the form of nodes (vertices), edges, and properties. When creating a node, you would give this node properties, then any edges used could also have properties. This helps build up a graph of data that is related directly to the data, rather than in rows with join tables as you would in a relational database.

Visually, you could interpret a graph database as a kind of web. Although you can have a graph database without any edges, more often than not, it will have them, and lots of them. A good example of a graph database in the physical world would be a crime diagram from a TV show, or of course in real life if you happen to have seen one.

With the crime diagram, suspects are related to other suspects, or the victim, and various bits of evidence are related for various reasons. This could be easily replicated in a graph database format, as it's just a big graph. The nodes in this case would be your evidence items and suspects, and they could connect together for various reasons, which would be logged via properties. Those who know of Breaking Bad, may remember Figure 1-4, but for those that haven't seen the show, or can't remember this particular scene, it's a crime diagram used in the show, which reminds me, SPOILER ALERT!

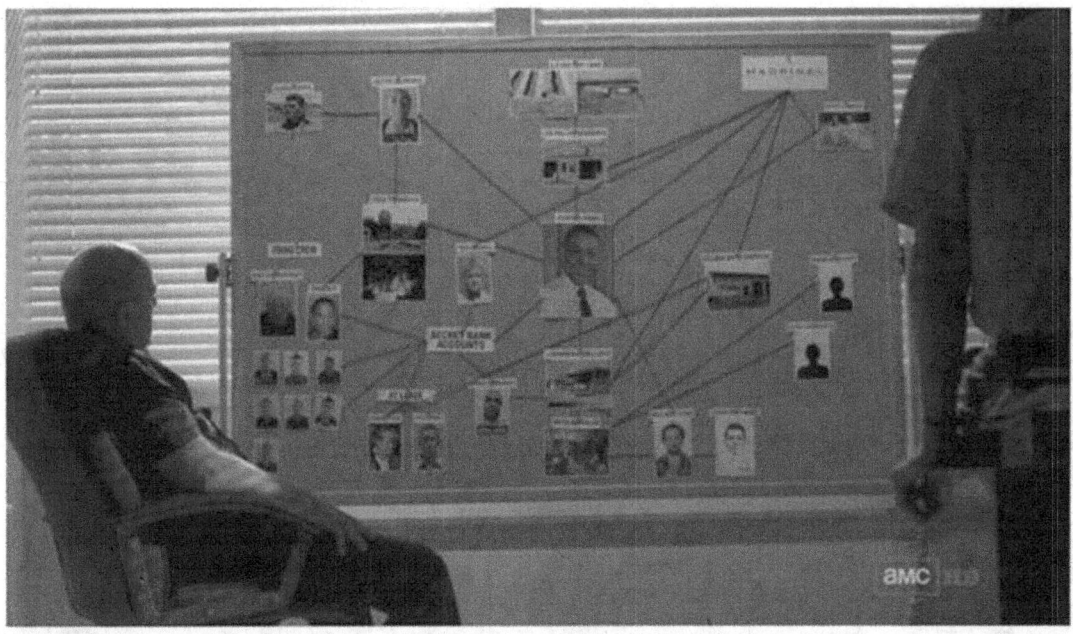

Figure 1-4. *A scene from Breaking Bad showing an evidence board, with connected people and evidence*

Another example of this is one from the TV show Heroes. The show aired in 2006 about ordinary people with extraordinary abilities (I loved that show) but it had a huge tie to the flow of time. If you haven't seen the show, or didn't care for it that isn't a problem, there's one example of a brilliant graph that's worth sharing either way.

In the show things start going wrong, so to help control this, one of the characters makes a physical timeline of events, featuring when events happened, who was involved, and how it was all related to any other event. This is very much like the previous example in that events would be classed as nodes, and the string connecting those nodes as edges. In Figure 1-5 you can see a portion of the graph from the show, where you can see the connections between different pictures and items on various bits of string.

Figure 1-5. *A still from Heroes, showing all of the characters lives and interactions represented with string and other items*

Depending on the graph database system you use, the language may change slightly, but it all comes down to vertices, nodes, and edges. As you'll soon learn Neo4j consists of Nodes, Relationships, and Properties, so here edges are relationships, and nodes are nodes. Titan DB on the other hand (another graph database) uses nodes and edges to describe its relationships. Although the terminology differs between the two, the underlying meaning is the same.

Of course in this case, there's only one graph database of interest, and that is Neo4j. Although the details of Neo4j will be explained in the next chapter, for now Neo4j uses Nodes, Properties, and Relationships (edges). As I said, different systems have different ways of wording the different elements, but it comes down to the same structure.

Relational Databases

Relational databases have been around for a while, and if you've ever used Drupal, WordPress, Magento, or a number of other applications, you'll have most likely used MySQL, which is a common relational database. MySQL is an example of a SQL (Structured Query Language) database, which stores its data in the form of tables, rows, and columns. This method of storing data is based on the relational model of data, as proposed by Edgar Frank Codd in 1970.

Within a relational database, you'll create a table for every type of data you want to store. So for example, a user table could be used to store user information, a movie table to store movies, and so on. Each row in an SQL table must have a primary_key which is the unique identifier for the row. Typically, this is an ID field that will automatically increment as rows are added. Using this system for storing data does work quite well, and has for a very long time, but when it comes to adding in relationships, that's when the problems potentially start.

If you've ever had to spend time in Excel, or another spreadsheet application, then you know how relational databases work, at least on some level. You'll set up your columns and then add rows that correspond to those columns. Although you can do a lot of other things in these applications, such as adding up all of the values in a column, the concept is the same. Excel at least has multiple sheets, and in the context of the spreadsheet application, a sheet is like a table, where you'll have one main document (the database, in this case) with many sheets, containing main columns and rows, that may or may not be related.

Relationships

When creating a relationship in a relational database (or SQL database), you would create your two data types, such as `person` and `team`, and most likely have a joining table named something like `person_team`. In the joining table, the unique identifier used in each table will be added as a row in the joining table. For example, if a person with the ID of 1, is in the team with an ID of 2, then the row in the `person_team` table would be something like that shown in Table 1-1.

Table 1-1. *An example joining table between a person and a team*

person_id	team_id
1	1
1	2
2	3
4	3
5	2
6	3
7	1
8	1

This approach works when it comes to relating small amounts of data, but when you start having to do multiple joins for thousands of rows, it starts to become slow, and eventually, unusable. This is a huge problem for the amount of data stored these days, and how that data relates to other data. If your website gets hit with a large spike of traffic, you'll want to be able to scale your database to keep up. In most cases this'll be fine, but if there's a join-intensive query, then unless it's been heavily optimized, there are going to be problems when you compare that to how easily a graph database handles the same issue.

Origins

As I mentioned earlier, the model used was proposed by Edgar Frank Codd in 1970 while he was still working at IBM. In 1970, while working at IBM, Codd published "A Relational Model of Data for Large Shared Data Banks" which showed the potential of his data model. Despite his efforts to get IBM to implement his changes, they were slow to do so, and only started doing so when competitors did.

Although they were slow in adapting the changes, they eventually did begin to implement them, but because Codd himself wasn't involved with the process (and the team weren't familiar with his ideas), rather than using his own Alpha query language, the team created their own. The team created SEQUEL (Later renamed SQL) and because it was so superior to what was already out there, it was copied.

Since the term relational database was so new, a lot of database vendors ended up adding the term to their name because of its popularity, despite said systems not actually being, relational. To try to prevent this and reduce the number of incorrect uses of his model, Codd put together a list of 12 rules which would be true to any relational database.

NoSQL

When you talk about databases at all, you need to mention NoSQL, which can be interpreted as "Not only SQL" or "Not SQL", depending on the conext. Just to make things confusing. Some NoSQL databases can handle SQL based queries, whereas others cannot, so this can differ between different NoSQL databases. If you're in doubt, just check the official documentation. The name is also somewhat misleading anyway, as it should have been called something like, NoREL (No relations) as it goes away from the traditional relational data model, so technically speaking, Neo4j and graph databases in general, are a type of NoSQL database. You may notice with some NoSQL databases that the query language used is somewhat similar to SQL in how it's written, which can help developers feel at ease with a new query language. You'll notice this with Cypher (Neo4js's query language) a lot if you're from an SQL background, as there are noticeable similarities in the syntax of both.

Depending on the database used, the benefits can be slightly different. There are those that focus on being able to scale well (example) and others that aim for data consistency. When you scale up a database to meet demand, it'll create more instances (or copies) of it, so the load is shared between however many instances exist. An issue with this though, is that the databases won't communicate with each other, so if a change is made, it may be made on one database but not the others, making the data inconsistent. When scaling, NoSQL databases can use the "Eventual Consistency" model to keep their data correct. This means that if a change is made, eventually, the change will be mirrored to all of the databases, but until this happens, the data retrieved may be incorrect. This is also known as BASE transactions, or Basic Availability, Soft-state and Eventual consistency transactions, which essentially says, it's available (so it scales, and data can be accessed) and it'll eventually be fully consistent, but this can't be guaranteed.

Back in 1998, Carlo Strozzi used the term NoSQL to describe an open source database he was working on, as it went away from the typical relational-database model by not exposing SQL to the user. Although this was the first time the term was used (purely because of its lack of SQL) it wasn't like the NoSQL databases we know now. Strozzi's database was still relational, whereas typically, NoSQL databases aren't.

The term stuck however, and then led to a new breed of databases that decided to go against the then-standard relational model. It would be a bit broad to have every database that wasn't relational under the same umbrella without some categorization, so the main types are key-value, column, document, and (you guessed it) graph.

Key Value

Given its name, you'd be right to assume that this is in fact, key-basedvalue storage. Essentially, you don't get a table, you don't get columns in the sense of a relational database, instead the database is like one big table, with many columns, or keys. Values are stored within the database using a key, and are retrieved using that key. This makes it a lot simpler than a traditional SQL driven database, and for some web applications, this is more than enough.

This approach does work for a lot of cases when your data isn't related, or especially structured but that's not always the case. This database approach is good if you just want to store a chunk of data you don't need to query against. You could, for example, store some JSON within a key-value store, but until it was retrieved from the database, you wouldn't be able to query against or use the data in any way.

Column

The column type of NoSQL database holds many similarities to the key-value based NoSQL database, in that it is still stored and retrieved using a key. The difference is that each column in the database consists of a key, value, and a timestamp. This is especially useful when scaling, as the timestamp can be used to work out which content is stale when the database is updated.

Document-orientated

Technically speaking, a document-orientated NoSQL database is actually a key-value based database, just a little bit more intelligent. The key-value style of the database is still respected, but in this case, the value is a structured document, rather than just text, or a single value. This means thanks to the increased structure of the information, the database will be able to perform more optimized queries, as well as making data retrieval easier in general.

Documents can be technically anything, depending on the database vendor's preference. One popular choice is JSON, which isn't the best for structuring data, but it allows the data to be used by both back- and front-end applications.

Graph

The graph style of NoSQL database is different still, and stores its content in the format of Nodes, Properties, and Edges. Throughout the course of the book, there will be a lot of talk on graph databases, as Neo4j is of course one. For now though, it's good to note that despite being a graph database, it's still a type of NoSQL database.

Summary

In this chapter lots of different database information has been covered, but things will move on from here. You always need to know the theory about something before you can properly use whatever it is you're learning, and that's what this chapter is all about. It shows that something conceived as early as 1736 by the brilliant Leonard Euler may still not see the light of day until the technology exists to make it happen.

When you talk about databases, you can never discount relational ones, and of course, this chapter was no exception. Relational databases have been around for some time now, mainly due to the abundance of resources to help you, and web applications that utilize them. Although they also relate data, this can come at a cost when relationships become complex, as you have more and more tables to join. Graph databases put relationships first, which means complex relationships are possible, without compromising performance.

There are many alternative databases out there, but each one has a different purpose, including Neo4j. We'll be relating a lot of data together in this both, crafting recommendations, and much more. Although I've only just touched on Neo4j, there is a whole chapter on its terminology, internals, and generally how it works, so don't worry if it's something new for you.

CHAPTER 2

■ ■ ■

Getting to Know Neo4j

Now that we've been over the theory of the various types of database, and even had a bit of a history lesson on the origins of graph theory, it's time to get into the good stuff, Neo4j. This chapter will give you a full overview on Neo4j, how it works, who's using it, and of course, why you should be using it. To kick things off, let's get a bit of information about Neo4j, and have a look at why you should be using it.

Neo4j is an open-source project, backed by Neo Technology which started back in 2003, with the application being publicly available since 2007. You can install Neo4j on Windows, OS X, or Linux so you can pretty much install it wherever you like, provided the machine meets the minimum requirements. The minimum requirements are detailed in the "Under the hood" section of this chapter.

The source code and issue tracker are available on GitHub so the community can help with the development of the product. There is an enterprise option of the application which has additional features, support, and is essentially a different product. This version is also closed-source, so it's only available when you pay for the license. You would only need to use the Enterprise edition if you had a very large Neo4j-backed application, and would be more comfortable having dedicated support. There is also a free Personal license which is applicable if you're in a company that has less than three employees, you are self-funded, and don't have more than US$100K in annual bookings. Essentially, if you're working on some kind of small application, you'll be fine with the personal license.

The current release (2.2.5) shows a great improvement over previous versions with speed increases, reliability increases, an optimized browser, faster Cypher queries, and a fancy new logo which can be seen in Figure 2-1. This will be the version used throughout the book, so in newer versions there may be some differences in the user interface and functionality, but wherever possible, I'll be trying to keep everything as relevant as possible. Technical books have to deal with this issue a lot, where versions change, and after the time of printing sometimes the code samples no longer work. To try and keep these instances down to a minimum I'll be hosting certain code samples and code online, so that if changes do happen the hosted code can be updated, to help keep things relevant. In the cases where this is applicable throughout the book, where the code can found will be made clear as and when it's needed.

Figure 2-1. *The new logo for Neo4j as of the 2.2.0 release*

Neo4j has always touted itself as "the World's Leading Graph Database" (it's even in the website title) and based on the releases mentioned on their website, they seem to put out new versions of the site every month on average. The 2.0 release came out back in 2013 and since then, they'd been maintaining the 1,9.* version of the application (which now sits as version 1.9.9, and is not recommended for use, but is still available) as well as the new version. This shows the software is being frequently updated with bug fixes and optimizations. You can read more about the different releases at http://neo4j.com/release-notes should you be interested.

Although the release history is good to know, it's not what's most important here. We're here to talk about the current release (2.2.5) so let's get on with that, shall we?

Give Me a REST

To communicate with Neo4j, you use its REST API via HTTP. For those unfamiliar with what REST is, then this is for you. Representational state transfer, or REST is a style used when designing network applications, and in pretty much all cases, HTTP is used to send the needed data to the application. When an application implements this protocol, it uses the HTTP verbs: GET, PUT, POST, and DELETE to perform certain actions within the application. In a nutshell this is how REST works, and it's what Neo4j uses to manage its data. This is just a heads up if you see REST later in the book and aren't sure what it is.

Why Choose Neo4j?

Of course there are a lot of reasons to use Neo4j, some of which I'll explain in a bit more detail, and a few others that are just worth mentioning. Neo4j has a huge community built around its 1,000,000+ downloads (which is mentioned on the website as one off the top 10 reasons to use it), and that figure is growing every month. They're also able to boast 500+ Neo4j events a year, 20,000+ meetup members, and a whole lot more.

These organized meetups mean that all over the world there are people who are passionate about Neo4j and want to talk about it, or so the website claims. Technology-based Meetups (whether it's about Neo4j, or any other technology) allow you to get insight into new techniques, use cases, examples, or even ideas that you had never thought of. When you're in a room with a lot of like-minded people, everyone is able to help each other and share ideas, you never know what'll happen when you go to a meetup.

Since 2000, Neo4j has been growing into its position as the top graph database on the web today, and there's a lot of work that's gone into getting it that far. Now, some 15 years later, Neo4j is a hugely dependable product offering scaling capabilities, incredible read and write speed, and of course full ACID compliance.

One of the big benefits of Neo4j (which will be seen as we go through the book) is that it's easy to pick up and learn. Although it'll be covered below, the query language, Cypher, has been designed to be descriptive to make it easier to understand, and also to learn. The Neo4j team has also published a number of helpful articles on different use cases for Neo4j, with how-to guides included. These can be found on their website, should you want to take a look.

When you're building an application around a particular technology, you want to have confidence that you'll be able to host said technology and that it'll be able to cope with the large amount of traffic you're application will get (we can all dream for that, right?), and Neo4j is no exception. This is reliant on two factors though, Neo4j itself and where it's hosted. Hosting options for Neo4j will be covered in Chapter 9, so you'll be able to learn more about the hardware side of things there, but as long as you have a solid hosting platform, Neo4j is designed to deal with large amounts of traffic.

In addition to many other features, Neo4j offers cluster support and high availability (HA) which means that, thanks to its master/slave design and its ability to propagate changes between the other instances in the cluster, your application will not only stay up under pressure, it'll be fast too.

Cypher

When the developers behind Neo4j were working on the query language to power it, they wanted something easy to use and easy to read. As mentioned above, Cypher was designed to be easy to read, and is described as "like SQL a declarative, textual query language" on the Neo4j website. The reasoning for developing Cypher this way comes down to ease of use, but also to help those coming from an SQL background feel more at ease using a non-SQL-like database. There's a full chapter dedicated to Cypher and all of its glory, so there won't be too much detail here, but you can't mention the reasons for choosing Neo4j without mentioning Cypher.

To make things as easy as possible, Cypher queries are descriptively written, and when the syntax finally clicks it makes it so easy to familiarize yourself with how it all fits together. When I was first using Cypher, I had to keep referring to the documentation to see where I was going wrong, but eventually it clicked and all made sense. We'll be going into a lot more detail about how Cypher works in a later chapter, so more complex actions will be covered for there. As with everything it's best to start with the basics. The basic Cypher syntax is as follows:

```
() Node
{} Properties
[] Relationships
```

These can be combined in a number of ways to achieve different queries. When searching through data, adding a property can filter the result set down, based on the value of that property. The same can be said for relationships, adding a relationship constraint to a query can give a more relevant and condensed result set, rather than seeing everything. One basic query that you may use a lot (I know I do) is:

```
MATCH (n) RETURN n;
```

This query returns every node in the database, which in the query itself is aliased with `n`. When I say every node, I do mean that, so it's advisable that you only run this on local environments, and not in production. If you ran this on a database with millions of nodes, it would take a long time and could also block some important transactions from happening. A property constraint could have to be added to the query to make it return a smaller subset of results, but sometimes, you just like to look at all the nodes in the graph. Using constraints would be recommended if are querying data on a large database to reduce to load time and make your result set smaller.

Relationships are one of the things Cypher tried to keep simple. It was also important to make the query language look descriptive, which you can see in the following query.

```
MATCH (a)-[:CONNECTED]->(b) RETURN a, b;
```

This query illustrates getting all nodes that are related to each other by the `CONNECTED` relationship, and then returning these nodes for use somewhere else. The main thing about relationships is the direction, illustrated by the --> in the above. In the example it's looking for any nodes related to any other nodes by that relationship, so depending on your dataset, that could be a lot of nodes. In this case though, any node `a` with an directed relationship `CONNECTED` to another node `b`. There are multiple ways this could be made more specific, such as searching for nodes with a specific label, or a specific property.

Although this overview is quite basic, it should hopefully give a taste of what Cypher can do, but also how easy it is to use, even with something like relationships. In the coming chapters, there will be a more detailed overview on Cypher itself, how to use it, and some of the more complex operations it's capable of. It's still possible to see that thanks to the way it's written, it makes the learning curve quite low, so you can be working on complex queries quickly. The use of Cypher also goes hand in hand with Neo4j's Browser, which is amazing, and a very powerful tool when it comes to learning the language. With that being said, let's talk about the Browser.

Browser

With the release of 2.2.0 came a new version of the Browser bundled with Neo4j (as shown in Figure 2-2). Before the update it was nice, but the improved design, layout, and speed make it so much better. The browser gives you the ability to query your database using Cypher, where you'll be able to view live results.

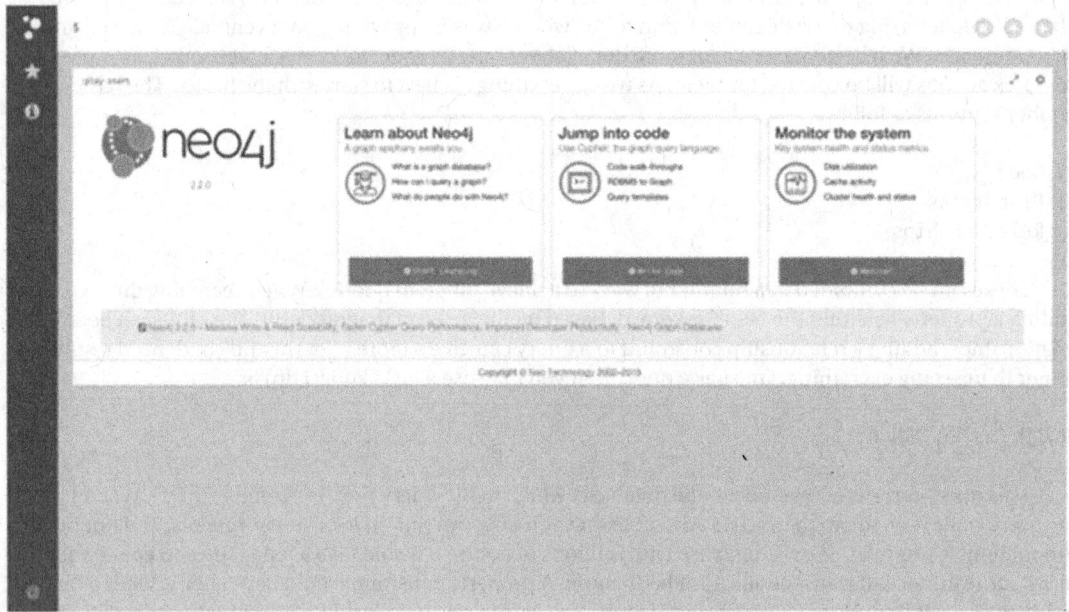

Figure 2-2. *The screen that greets you when you navigate to the Neo4j browser*

Working this way offers a number of advantages, including instant feedback, so if you make a mistake, you know what went wrong. The results returned from these queries can be seen in a graph (if applicable) or as a list of results. Each of these has their advantages, being able to see the graph allows you to see relationships, and potentially modify your query to make it more optimized.

When you set up Neo4j, you'll have a blank database, but to make the process of learning Cypher easier, a number of sample graphs are included within the browser that you can load in and experiment with. One of these graphs is the movie graph, which is provided by the lovely people at Neo Technology, and is simple to install. You can type `:play movie graph` to view the instructions required to load in this data into your database.

To demonstrate what the different result types look like, I'll be running `MATCH (n) RETURN n;` against this database. If you have access to Neo4j (installation instructions are available in Chapter 3) I'd advise you do the same. Whether you're performing the query yourself, or just following along (which is of course perfectly fine) then the results will look similar to Figure 2-3.

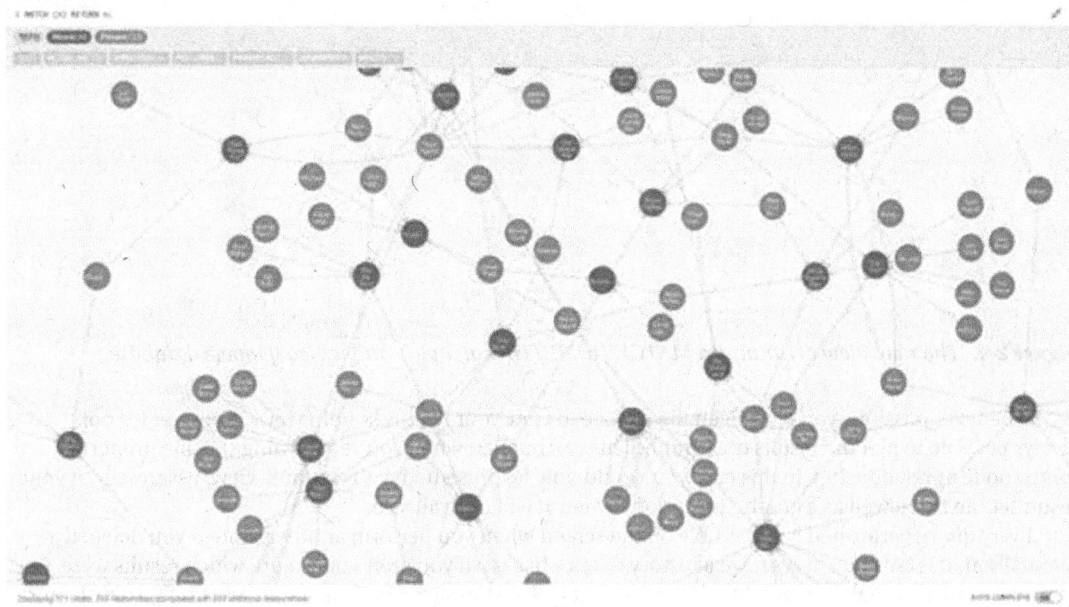

Figure 2-3. *The graph view of running a MATCH (n) RETURN n; query on the Neo4j movie database*

Although you can't see it from Figure 2-3, the result graph is very interactive. You can click on Nodes to get their individual properties, relationships, and an overview of your data. You can also see labels attached to nodes, and different labels can even be color coded to make it easier. If a node has multiple relationships, the graph will do its best to make these all visible, although some overlapping can occur if there are a lot of nodes. To make things even easier, you can also change the color or size of a relationship or node to make things easier to distinguish.

In Figure 2-4 you can see the list view with no display options, just data. The list view allows you to see all of the properties associated with your nodes, in a more traditional table-style layout. If you have a lot of data in your database, being able to see queries in this way is better because it allows you to see all of the properties of your returned nodes at a glance.

Figure 2-4. *The rows view of running a MATCH (n) RETURN n; query on the Neo4j movie database*

Whenever possible, you'll be given the chance to view your results in both views; however it's not always possible to plot the results on a graph. This can happen when you're returning specific properties from a node or relationship. In this case you would only be presented with the table view. Essentially, if your result set can be viewed as a graph, the option to view it will be available.

Every query performed is still visible on the screen when you perform another (unless you delete it manually, that is) so you always have a history to refer back to if you aren't quite sure which results were returned from a particular query. In addition, you can also stop slow/inefficient queries (that's a new feature as of 2.2.0) so that it doesn't crash the application. You can also export the graph in a number of formats, including SVG, CSV, JSON, and PNG, if you want to export that set of results, or use it in a presentation. You can also export the table-based output as a CSV or JSON.

The browser allows you to easily interact with Cypher so you could create your entire data structure from the browser. Having the browser can be useful when hosting Neo4j, as it allows you to interact with your data easily, directly from the browser. It also contains a number useful links, the option to read tutorials, manage user settings, and more. You can also save queries for later if you have certain ones you like to run more often, or to make running a demo easier.

Thanks to Neo4j's REST interface (which will be covered in just a moment) you may never need to use the browser, but it's a great resource, especially when learning. It's useful to use when texting queries that are going to be used in applications, as it gives not only the query results, but also shows any errors, and provides the execution time, so if a query is running a bit slow, you can tweak it in the browser to get it right, then put it in your application.

If you run a system with registrations or user-created content, being able to quickly jump into the browser and run a simple query allows you to see new registrants, new nodes/relationships, and more. You could even save these queries for later use (using the star icon) to make it even easier. If you want to use the result for something, then you can just export it into the previously mentioned formats, nice and simple.

Webadmin

Another interface available through the browser is webadmin, which can be found by clicking the information icon in the sidebar and then clicking the "Webadmin" link at the bottom of the panel. This is essentially an administration section for Neo4j, where it's possible to view rough stats, check configuration values, and much more. For most beginners, this section won't really be of much use, but knowing it's there and what it can be do is useful.

When you first navigate to webadmin (`http://localhost:7474/webadmin/`) you'll be presented with a presentation about the features available within the section, should you need it. If not though, it can be closed and you'll gain access to the first tab, the dashboard. If you close it accidentally, or you'd like to have another look at the guide, a link to it is available from the top-right corner of the screen.

On the dashboard you'll be able to see some statistics about your database; however it's worth noting these values are approximate because this data is intended to give a status of the system, rather than giving exact stats. Either way, you can see counts for: nodes, properties, relationships, relationship types, and approximate values for database disk usage and logical log disk usage.

In addition, you get access to a graph for the counts of the nodes, properties, and relationships, which can be broken down into various time increments. This allows you to see the growth (or fall, if your application removes values) of the values within your database, and also a breakdown of when certain spikes or surges occur. When trying to debug issues, or gain additional insight into your application, being able to see at a minimum the last 30 minutes' values, right up to a years' worth of data is useful.

That's just the dashboard! The webadmin also allows you to interact with Neo4j in a number of ways, including easily updating node values, indexes, and more. You can also gain access to the configuration values being used for Neo4j, the underlying JVM, and more. This section within the browser provides multiple means of access to your data and easy interfaces for updating values. Although a beginner may not use this tool much, it has many features, and Neo4j allows you to overview the configuration straight from the browser, rather than having to access the server directly.

Under the hood

To make an application this universal and powerful, you need to use a quality tool. In this case, Neo Technology opted for Java, well, Java 7 to be precise. Java has been around for at least 20 years, and the fact it tries to make it so its developers will write the code once, and (hopefully) run it anywhere, makes Neo4j's cross-platform nature a lot easier. I could very easily go into a lot of detail about Java; however for the purposes on Neo4j, or at least the beginning aspects of it, all that needs to be taken from the use of JVM (Java Virtual Machine) is that it's a good choice.

To make the building of the various applications Neo4j is responsible for easier, it also utilizes Apache Maven. Apache Maven is an open-source project management tool that makes aspects of the managing the codebase for the project a lot easier.

The browser that comes with Neo4j is built using Node.js which is built on Google Chrome's Javascript engine, and is fast, lightweight, and efficient. Using Neo4j's REST interface allows the browser to interact with the data within Neo4j really easily. It's good to see that the browser is built using the same REST interface that anybody has access to in Neo4j, so if you wanted to, you could build your own browser.

With all of these specs you'd think you'd need a beast of a machine, and if you go off the recommended specifications, you'd be correct. If you're going to be processing a huge database, then you'll need a pretty powerful machine, the specs of which can be seen in Table 2-1.

Table 2-1. *The minimum and recommended specifications for Neo4j*

Requirement	Minimum	Recommended
CPU	Intel Core i3	Intel Core i7
Memory	2GB	16—32GB or more
Disk	10GB SATA	SSD w/ SATA
Filesystem	ext4 (or similar)	ext4, ZFS

The specs themselves aren't actually too bad, part of the use of Java requires a bit more RAM than normal for caching and other operations, and the better CPU is for better graph computation, so they're reasonable recommendations. The recommended disk is an SSD to increase the speed of reads and writes, and the filesystem needs to be ext4 or ZFS (Standard in UNIX based filesystems) to ensure it can be fully ACID compliant, because they take advantage of ext4 and ZFS ACID-compliant writes. Compared to some, this application isn't as hungry, and this level of specification is only needed if Neo4j is going to be powering a large amount of data, and handling a lot of operations.

Who's Using it?

With Neo4j launching back in 2003, you can imagine that there are a number of people using it by now, and you'd be correct! With downloads for this graph database now over a million, among all of those downloads are some high-profile clients, such as Ebay, Walmart, and Cisco. In these cases each of the clients, high profile or not, happen to have their own use case for Neo4j, be it for recommendations or social aspects, and Neo4j is the tool for the job. Some of the other companies said to be using Neo4j (according to the Neo4j website) are as follows:

- onefinestay
- Zephyr Health
- FiftyThree
- Gamesys
- Lufthansa Systems
- Wanderu
- Tomtom
- Telenor
- Infojobs
- Zeebox
- classmates
- spring
- HP
- National Geographic

Social and recommendation aspects aren't the only reasons to use Neo4j. Clients also boast being able to use it for Fraud Detection, Identity and Access management, Data management, and more. This is of course a small subset of actual clients and use cases, and with 200 enterprise subscription customers, including 50+ of the Global 2000, there is certainly no shortage in companies, big or small, that see Neo4j as the solution to their various graph database problems. For more information on Neo4j users, go to http://neo4j.com/customers/.

Indexes

If you're from the database world at all, then you'll know about an index. A database index is a copy of information in the database for the sole purpose of making retrieving said data more efficient. This does come at the cost of additional storage space and slower writes. With Neo4j, an index can be created for a particular property on a node, that has a certain label. Applying the index is done using the following query:

```
CREATE INDEX ON :Person(name)
```

This query will make an index on all of the name properties for any node with the label `Person` so if that query is one that is used often in your code, then this will be a lot faster. To save on speed, when Neo4j adds an index, it is not immediately available, and will be added in the background. When the index is ready, it'll be automatically used within your existing queries if it's possible to do so.

Being able to use indexes in this way means you can monitor your application for potential places for improvement, and then apply an index to help speed up the operation. The index will also be kept up to date without any additional maintenance, so if it's done correctly you'd just apply an index, forget about it, then reap the sweet optimized rewards. For some reason though, an index may not be working out for you. If that's the case, an index can easily be dropped. Again with no change to any existing code, Neo4j will work out whether an index is applicable to use by itself. There will be a more in-depth look at indexes in Chapter 4, this was just a brief overview to show that indexes are available within Neo4j, and are easy to use.

Caching

To help Neo4j be as fast as possible, two different caching systems are used: a file buffer cache and an object cache. These two systems have very different roles. The file buffer cache is intended to speed up queries by storing a copy of the information retrieved from the graph, whereas the object cache stores optimized versions of nodes, properties, and relationships to speed up graph traversal.

File Buffer Cache

When data is returned from the database, it's then stored in the cache in the same format, so if the same data is asked for again, it can be quickly retrieved. In addition when writing to the cache, each action is written to the transaction log, so if something does happen, Neo4j's ACID nature will stop this from being written, and the data will be available in the logs for recovery. This however is just an edge case as the cache is perfectly safe to use, and gives a speed increase as a bonus. The cache will also try and optimize things where it can as well. For example, if lots of small transactions are taking place, these will be combined to have fewer page rights, and therefore, you guessed it, more speed.

Of course you can't just cache the whole database, but that would take up a lot of storage, and that just isn't a viable option, so to avoid this, you'll set a cache limit. The more cache you have, the more space it'll take up, so essentially the bigger the cache you have, the more disk space you require. This can then have additional cost constraints if you're hosting provider is capped by size because increasing the limit usually results in an increased cost.

Data stored within the cache isn't always needed. Sometimes an action may be a one-off, whereas other repeated actions remain uncached. To get around this, Neo4j will keep an eye on the size of the cache, when it begins to reach capacity, it'll swap out old, unused items with better ones that will make the system faster. It's all very clever.

Depending on your needs, it's possible to change the amount of space dedicated to this cache. Since the data in this cache is stored within RAM, it's not always possible to dedicate large amounts to it; however, it cannot be disabled, so it's highly recommended you have at least a few megabytes dedicated to it. Although it's a useful cache to have enabled, it's good to know you can strip its RAM dependency right down, especially on systems where there isn't a lot of RAM available.

Object Cache

The other caching system within Neo4j is the object cache, which allows for fast traversal of the graph and is split into two types: reference caches and high-performance caches. The reference cache system utilizes the fact it's built on Java to maximize as much of the JVM heap memory as possible. Now this could be a very greedy process, but luckily, the cache is the lowest rung in the ladder, and will only maximize its use of the heap memory if it's safe to do so. Essentially, any shared applications running on the same JVM aren't using it, and Neo4j itself doesn't need it for anything else, so on that side, it keeps itself clean.

The cache system itself stores nodes and their relationships, so with this cache in place, if you've done a lookup already and the data hasn't changed, the query will hit the cache and give a response immediately, just as you'd expect from a cached system.

High-performance Cache

The other variant of the object cache, high-performance, is only available in the Enterprise edition of Neo4j, and stores nodes, their relationships, and their properties. This on the surface sounds great, if there's more stuff in the cache, then that makes everything faster, right? Although this can be the case, it won't always be. This caching system relies heavily on Java's garbage collection to ensure the cache doesn't get too large. Although this cache can be very powerful, it's one that must be monitored to ensure there weren't any large pauses or performance losses when the caches were cleared.

Extending Neo4j

It's possible to add additional functionality to Neo4j with the use of plugins. If there is a particular bit of functionality you want in Neo4j, there may be well be a plugin for it, or if you're feeling up to the task, you could write the plugin yourself. One of the more popular plugins is the Spatial plugin, which extends Neo4j to allow it to do location-based queries. This gives some very powerful functionality to Neo4j, by exposing a series of location-based tools and shows the power of plugins and how extendable Neo4j is.

Plugins can be installed in a variety of ways, depending on how they're built. For example, the Spatial plugin can be installed using Apache Maven, as well as being placed in the plugins directory (/var/lib/neo4j/plugins, if you've installed in the default location) directly. Although plugins can be installed in a number of ways, the fact that it's possible to use them in the first place is the main thing.

Summary

This chapter provided more insight into Neo4j and some of its many features. As the book progresses, a number of these features will be explained in more detail, especially Cypher since it's Neo4j's query language and will be used to interact with Neo4j throughout the book. Not only is Neo4j currently boasting a new release, 1,000,000+ downloads, and more than 10 years in production, it has also made a solid place for itself in the market, that isn't going to change any time soon.

   With its ever-growing time in production, the community, and resources for the community continue to grow, if you ever have a query, StackOverflow, the Google group, or even the dedicated support staff at Neo Technologies can help. If you're having a problem, odds are that someone has had that problem before, so have a search and you may well find your answer. Failing that, if you create a post on either StackOverflow or the Google group, somebody will be able to help you.

   A very brief look at Cypher has shown the potential power it has as a language, and how easy it is to use. The descriptive nature of the query language keeps it easy to pick up, and you can try and much as you like in Neo4j's browser, using the demo data, or your own. The browser is a brilliant accompaniment to an equally brilliant platform, and adds a set of tutorial and data-management tools, as well as the console where you can interact with your Neo4j data live, with the chance to view the results in table or graph format.

   We've talked enough about why Neo4j is good to use, and have also learned a bit more about it in this chapter. Now, it's time to actually get Neo4j up and running on your system, which is covered in the next chapter.

■ ■ ■

CHAPTER 3

Get Up and Running with Neo4j

Things are starting to get interesting now. We've been over a bit of history, and then got to know Neo4j a little better as well, now it's time to get started. To start taking advantage of the awesome things Neo4j has to offer, we need to install it first. Whether you use Windows, Mac, or Linux, getting started with Neo4j is really easy. On any of these systems, it's possible to install Neo4j directly, or potentially by using Vagrant, which is a tool used to create development environments. If you're unfamiliar with Vagrant, don't worry, everything will be explained soon enough.

■ **Note** Not everybody likes to use virtual environments so to cover all bases whether you use Windows, a Mac, or a flavor of Linux, all of those installation instructions will be covered. If you're going with a direct approach, then regardless of your operating system, you'll need to download the code from neo4j.com, so to avoid repetition, let's get to that. There is also an option to build Neo4j from source, so if you're interested in doing that, head to the Neo4j github page (github.com/neo4j/neo4j) and you can follow the helpful instructions in their README.md file.

Downloading from Neo4j.com/download

You can use the package downloaded from the Neo4j website regardless of your operating system, however in the case of Ubuntu it's actually easier to install it using a package. The option to install via the website is still there, so it's worth covering.

When you head to the page, you can choose from a number of options, most of which are about which of the editions to download. The option to go for here is the Community edition, unless you're willing to dive into the 30-day free trial for the Enterprise edition, that is. Once you've hit the conveniently large green button, you'll be taken to a download page and your download will start automatically, with a link if it doesn't work.

Windows users actually get a rather easy installation process, as you actually just receive an .exe file that does all of the hard work for you, but we'll go through that in a moment. For Mac and Unix, what you're downloading is a zipped Neo4j environment, ready to run and essentially all you have to do is start the server. Before you can do that though, you'll have to make sure you have either Oracle JDK 7 or Open JDK 7 installed. In this case JDK stands for Java Development Kit, and in this case, it's for the Standard Edition.

Conveniently enough, there are actually links to both of these on the download page, which makes things a little easier, although there are alternatives available, which we'll cover on a per-OS basis.

Once JDK is sorted, you can theoretically run the server, and you'll be ready to go. Since the steps can be different per system, those will be covered separately, starting with Windows.

Installing on Windows

Installing directly on Windows couldn't be easier, as the download you receive from the Neo4j website does everything, including dealing with the JDK dependency. If you're running Windows Enterprise edition, you will need to install JDK, but as mentioned above, you can find a link to that from the download page above. In this case, I'm installing on clean version of Windows 10, but these instructions should also work on other versions, too. If in doubt, check the Neo4j website. Anyway, back to business, this easy installation results in you being able to double click the .exe file to install everything, which is brilliant. You'll be guided through the installation process and you'll be prompted to pick an installation location, and after the process is complete, you'll get the option to run Neo4j.

When you run Neo4j, you'll see a dialog similar to that in Figure 3-1. The only difference potentially being the path of the database.

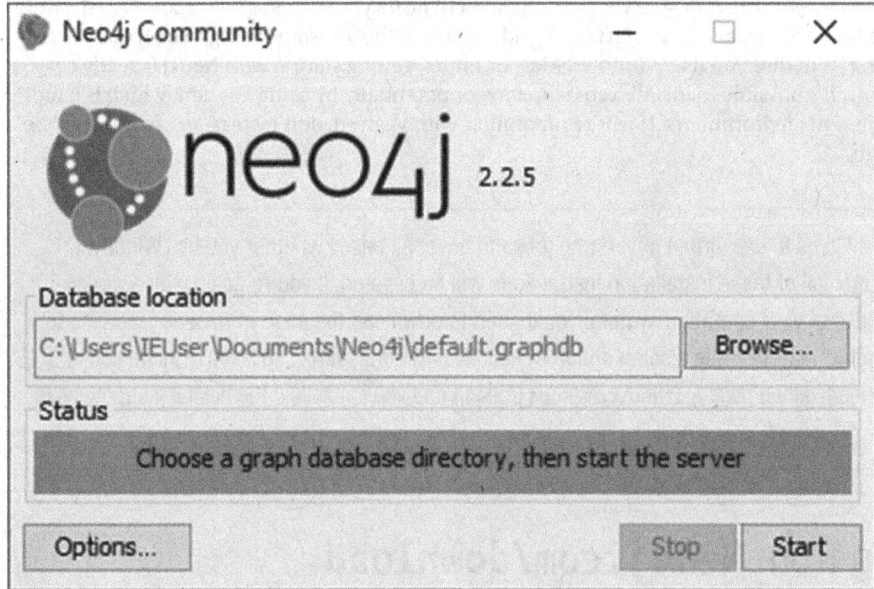

Figure 3-1. *The dialog visible when you start Neo4j on Windows 10*

To start the server, just hit the button, then the dialog will change, and the server will be available at `http://localhost:7474`, which will be shown in the dialog. You're now up and running with Neo4j, nice and easy!

Installing on Mac

For the sake of keeping things even, this installation will take place on a clean Mac with OS X Yosemite (Version 10.10.3, to be exact) which comes with Java installed, but in this case, that's not what's needed. Sadly, there aren't any easy shortcuts to getting installed on a Mac, it pretty much just comes down to downloading Neo4j, and ensuring your system is able to run it. As I mentioned earlier, you'll need JDK 7 to run Neo4j, so the first thing to do is check the version you have installed, which you can do via your favorite Terminal application, and pressing:

```
java -version
```

This will tell you the version you have installed, if any. If your version isn't 1.7, then you'll need to install the correct version in order for Neo4j to run. There are a couple of approaches that can be used here: installing direct via the one of the links from the Neo4j download page, or by using Homebrew. As both are perfectly reasonable choices, and I don't want to force my will on you (I like the Homebrew option) we'll go through both, starting with going direct.

Installing from a Website

This approach uses one of the previously mentioned links from the Neo4j download page. It doesn't matter which approach you go for, but the easier of the two is the Oracle approach, purely because the link provided takes you to the correct place on the website. You'll need to accept the user agreement for Java SE Development Kit, then download the version for OS X. The file you download is a DMG, so just follow the steps and you'll soon have JDK installed. One alternative is to use Homebrew, which we'll go through now.

Going with Homebrew for Java

If you're unsure of what Homebrew is, or you're fan of it and like being reminded how great it is, then let's address both, shall we? Homebrew is a package manager for OS X, which makes installing missing packages from your system easy as pie. One of the first packages I'd always install is the demo one they use, wget. Homebrew's tagline is "The missing package manager for OS X."

Essentially, there are a lot of smaller packages that you may need as a developer, and installing them manually is a pain (wget being a great example) so Homebrew tries to make that easier. Each package is stored in its own location on your system, so it can be just as easily removed as it is installed, plus, this means that if there's a bug in a package you've downloaded, you can update it, brilliant! Of course, Homebrew takes care of maintaining the packages. You just install or manage them via commands, it's easy! The good thing is, you can search Homebrew for different packages as well, so before trying to build something from source or using an installer, check if Homebrew has a tap for it (tap being what they call their package repositories).

Enough chat, let's install it, which is nice and easy, so there's nothing to worry about. To get the code needed, it's best to head over to the website and ensure it's correct (it's right at the top), then paste the code into your Terminal window, and it should look something like this:

```
ruby -e "$(curl -fsSL https://raw.githubusercontent.com/Homebrew/install/master/install")
```

When you run the command, it'll give you step by step instructions on how to install it, and soon enough you'll be done, and ready to move onto the next step, installing Homebrew Cask.

Homebrew Cask

The concept of having a decent package manager on your Mac is great, but one for your extensions is even better, and Homebrew Cask, is what you're looking for. As I briefly mentioned earlier, Homebrew Cask is an extension of Homebrew, taking the concept and applying it to applications instead. The applications in question are open source and readily available, so you can't install Photoshop with it, essentially. You can also install things like Java with it, which is why I'm bringing it up now. As with Homebrew itself, you can just search an application (Google Chrome is a common one) and it'll install it for you, without you having to download anything from the website. Since the Java SDK can be installed this easily (it's just called Java, but it's actually the SDK) it's time to install Homebrew Cask and get moving. The code for Homebrew Cask is actually a cask, so installing it can be done like so:

```
brew install caskroom/cask/brew-cask
```

It's around about 50MB in total, so it may take a little time depending on your connection, but soon enough you'll have it installed, and now, it's FINALLY time to install Java. First, the version of Java in Cask may be wrong, so to fix that, run the following:

```
brew tap caskroom/versions
```

This updates the versions repository for Java from the caskroom, it'll download a tiny a package, then you can finally run:

```
brew cask install java7
```

This will install the missing Java version and allow you to finally run Neo4j, which is brilliant. Plus with it being managed by Homebrew it can be just as easily removed as it was installed, and it can be updated just as easily, which is brilliant.

With Java Installed

No matter how you've installed Java, it's now installed, which means Neo4j is finally ready to go. Now, all that needs to be done is to `cd` into where you have Neo4j on your system, and run the following:

```
./bin/neo4j console
```

This will run the Neo4j server, and it'll be available for you to see at http://localhost:7474 when it's finished doing its thing and prints `INFO [API] Remote interface ready and available at [http://localhost:7474/]` to show that it is. You can now have a chance to play with the Browser and get used to where everything is, which is good because you'll be in here a lot.

Now Neo4j is installed on your system and ready to use. Now, anytime you want to use Neo4j, just `cd` into the directory and run `./bin/neo4j console` then you're up and running. The first time you visit the Browser, you will be required to authorize the application by logging in, and then by changing your password. The default details are `username: neo4j` and `password: neo4j` but they're also shown on the screen when you need to login, so it's easy enough to follow along. Be sure to make a note of the new password, as this will be needed to authenticate any application that needs to access your data, so when using it in production, be sure it's a secure password.

Installing on Ubuntu

When it comes to installing on Ubuntu (or any other Debian based Linux distribution), there is actually a nice and easy way to get Neo4j installed, which is always a good thing. As mentioned earlier, you could of course use the package downloaded from the Neo4j website, and install Java 1.7, but because Ubuntu doesn't official support 1.7, it's a little awkward, but it is still possible. For ease though, we'll be running through the approach that uses Ubuntu's package manager, which means you can have Neo4j installed in a few lines. Let's get started.

The first thing that you'll need to do is open up a Terminal window, and type `sudo su` which will prompt you for the administrator password. This process logs you in as the root user on the machine which means all commands are run as root/admin. The commands that are required all require root access, so it essentially saves having to put `sudo` in-front of every command. With you now as the root user (there would have been some change to the prompt, potentially) the first command that needs to be run is:

```
wget -O - http://debian.neo4j.org/neotechnology.gpg.key | apt-key add -
```

This command adds the Neo4j repository key to the package manager, so that when we add where to download Neo4j from, it actually works, by signing the downloads correctly. When the command runs, it'll download the key from the Neo4j website, then pipe it into `apt-key` so it can be used. The next command on the list is adding where to get Neo4j from, which we do so by running:

```
echo 'deb http://debian.neo4j.org/repo stable/' > /etc/apt/sources.list.d/neo4j.list
```

Running this command will add the Neo4j repository location to the `apt` sources list, so when we go to install it, it'll now look for Neo4j in the correct place. One thing worth noting here is the word `stable`, as this refers to the build of Neo4j that will be downloaded, and is the recommended version to use. If desired it's also possible to use the `oldstable` or `testing` builds of Neo4j, but again, it's recommended that `stable` is used.

With the desired build added, there's only two steps left, update the system, then install Neo4j. Updating the system is easy, and can be done by:

```
apt-get update -y
```

This will install any updates to the system and check all of the repositories in the source list for any updates. When the command has finished, there's one more left, installing Neo4j, which is done with:

```
apt-get install neo4j -y
```

This will take care of downloading the files, and also installing everything. When everything is finished, the Neo4j Browser will be available to you at http://localhost:7474 just like the other solutions. The installation process has installed Neo4j as a service, and it'll now always run when you start the machine. You can of course start, stop, or even restart the service as often as you like, depending on preference. If you run `service neo4j-service` (or with sudo in front if you aren't still the root user) the following options are provided: start, stop, status, restart, and force-reload. So if you'd like to restart to the service, just run `service neo4j-service restart` (Don't forget about sudo, if you need it) and the service will restart itself.

As with the different build of Neo4j that could be used, there's also the different versions that can be installed as well. The version that has just been installed is the community addition, but advanced and enterprise editions can be installed with `apt-get install neo4j-advanced` and `apt-get install neo4j-enterprise` respectively.

With all of the steps done, that's it, Neo4j is installed on the system and is ready to use, and with it being installed through the package manager, it means that any updates that come through will automatically be applied, which is always nice.

Install Neo4j in a Vagrant Box

Vagrant is a system for provisioning your application, and allows it to run in a virtual server environment. This means that you have what would be a server, right on your local environment, which makes collaboration, debugging and management a lot easier. You also don't need to have just one Vagrant box either, multiple different versions can exist on your system. You can even create your own or use others from the community (I have one for Neo4j, for example) which makes being able to jump on and try a new technology a lot easier, because if somebody has already built a vagrant box for the software you want to use then it's less setup for you, which is great!

I could go on for ages about how good Vagrant is, but it's time to start getting it installed. There are a number of solutions you can use for creating virtual operating systems and of course Vagrant doesn't reinvent the wheel on this, it just utilizes those packages that exist, well Virtualbox and VMWare, that is.

If you're unfamiliar with these systems, they allow you to create a virtual environment on your host machine, so you could install Windows on your Mac, for example. Of all the packages it supports, Virtualbox is the favorite, as it's open source and cross platform, which makes it a good system to depend on.

Since we know Virtualbox is needed, it's time to install. If you head on over to `virtualbox.com` to download the latest version for your system. At the time of writing, Vagrant is version 1.7.4 and Virtualbox is supported for versions 4.0.x, 4.1.x, 4.2.x, 4.3.x, and 5.0.x. This pretty much means you should be good to go no matter what version you have, but it's always best to check the officially supported version on the `vagrantup.com` website before installing. You can of course install one of the other supported virtualization platforms, which will cause the configuration of the box to be different (we'll get to that soon) but it should function in the same way.

With the emulation stuff out of the way, it's time to install Vagrant itself, so you can now head over to `vagrantup.com` and downloaded the relevant installer for your system, and when it's all finished, there's only a couple more steps until you're up and running. The command to get everything started in Vagrant is to use `vagrant up` which will start an essentially empty server in the directory you use. With additional configuration in the Vagrant file, and the use of something to provision the box, like Puppet or Chef, then you'd have your ready to use server. Thanks to some Blue Peter style magic "Here's one I made earlier" as I've already created and configured a Vagrant box to run Neo4j, which you can get from:

```
https://github.com/chrisdkemper/neo4j-vagrant
```

Thanks to it being on Github it'll always get updated, so if any bugs come up, I can get them fixed, or if any updates come up (feel free to do a pull request) then just do a `git pull` and you'll be fine. Speaking of `git pull` you'll need Git to pull down the repository. If you aren't familiar with Git, it's a brilliant source control system, and you should really familiarize yourself with it, in case you need to use it. If you're new to Git, then there's a number of online resources to get you up to speed, but all you need to pull down from the repository is:

```
git clone https://github.com/chrisdkemper/neo4j-vagrant.git my-project
```

This will pull a copy of the code down to your location machine, and just change `my-project` to whichever folder name you'd like. Then when you're inside you can just do `git pull` to get any updates, and if you make no changes then that's it. You can of course change the name of the remote, and add a new one for your project code.

With the code now on your machine, all you have to do is run `vagrant up` and the box will begin provision, and when it's done the server is available at `http://localhost:7474`.

Summary

Depending on your choice of system, your installation process may have been a lengthy or short one, but either way Neo4j is up and running, and ready to use on your system. Now things are finally starting to get interesting, in the next chapter, we'll be taking a look at Cypher, and the commands you'll need to perform certain actions, which is just what you need to get up to speed with it and see how it works.

Although installing on your host system is perfectly fine, if you haven't tried Vagrant, I'd highly recommend it. I've of course given my Vagrant box repository as the example project, however you can use Vagrant to install anything you'd like. You can either write your own or use one from the community. It's a brilliant resource, and the more people use it (or something similar) the sooner we'll get rid of the whole "Well, it works on my machine" discussion, which has been going on a little long now.

■ ■ ■

CHAPTER 4

Meet Cypher

With Neo4j finally installed, it's time to get into the really interesting stuff, and start looking into its query language, Cypher. When I first heard Cypher, I actually thought of a certain Pokemon with knife hands that was green, wings, and is pretty cool. For those who aren't so into Pokemon, I'm referring to Syther. Name aside, Cypher really is a brilliant language, and when you get the hang of it, it's really easy to use.

This chapter will serve as a cheatsheet essentially, giving a rundown of the different commands and actions that can be performed, and the code needed to do them. With that out of the way, the next chapter is when things will start to get interesting, when we use the knowledge gained from this chapter, and apply it to actual data, to show the raw power Cypher has to offer.

Basic Syntax

When you perform a Cypher query, what you're actually doing is giving it pattern, and then Cypher will use that pattern to find data. With any other pattern, you'd need to use certain patterns and identifiers to find or match certain data, and of course Cypher is no exception. We've already seen the patterns needed to match Nodes, Relationships, and Properties previously, but it's time to go into a bit more detail.

In addition to the patterns themselves, one thing worth noting is the casing of the language. Throughout the book you'll see certain keywords (or clauses, as they're known in Cypher) written in uppercase. As with other languages (such as MySQL) the casing actually isn't important, but when you start writing more complex queries, having the clauses in capitals helps distinguish the different parts of the query. In this case, I'll be staying with uppercase as it helps to break the query up, and makes it easier to read. Values on the other hand are case sensitive. With that out of the way, it's time to cover how to use Nodes, Relationships, and Properties.

Before we go into the specifics of the different parts of the query, let's look at an example query, and break down the components of it to make going through it later easier. Since it was used previously we'll go with the following query:

```
MATCH (n) RETURN n;
```

The query in this case starts with MATCH which is a clause, and a query must start with one, so other possible options are CREATE and BLAH. If you didn't start with a clause, then Cypher wouldn't know what to do with the rest of the query, so just think of it as an instruction. We then have the node in its parentheses, aliased by `n`. Since there aren't any filters or property filters on this query (we'll get to those later in the chapter) then `n` actually represents every node in the database. The RETURN part of the query is what is actually returned, and since `n` is used again, then every node will be returned, and thanks to the query not being filtered this also brings back all of the properties and relationships tied to these nodes.

Most of the time when you're working with data, you'll have different types, and of course Neo4j is no different here so to distinguish types, Labels are used. A label is represented using a colon, followed by the name of the label and can only be applied to nodes. For example, if you were to use the previous query but you wanted to get all of the nodes labeled with `Product` it would be as follows:

```
MATCH (n:Product) RETURN n;
```

It's possible for a node to have multiple labels, and it's also possible to query against multiple labels, so if a `Promoted` label were to be introduced to certain products (in addition to the Product label) that could be represented like so:

```
MATCH (n:Product:Promoted) RETURN n;
```

Now only nodes with both labels will be returned. The previous query could well be written without the use of the `Product` label to only return the promoted products, but it does show how multiple labels can work together.

These were just a few examples to give an idea on the basic structure of a query to make things a bit easier going forward. There are still things such as Properties and Relationships to go over, but they'll be covered in isolation. With that out of the way let's take a more in-depth look at nodes.

Nodes

As you may recall, nodes are represented using parentheses (), so if you see them in a query, you know it's a node. In most cases you'd see a node with some kind of identifier inside it, but in some instances, if you don't care about the name (or alias) of the node(s) you're querying, it can actually be omitted. Most of the time, the node, or nodes that you are querying will most likely be used later in the query in some way, so having an alias makes sense. Of course, if you're for example, just creating multiple nodes, then you could leave out the alias if you wanted to, but it's entirely optional. Generally speaking, it's easier to keep the aliases in just to get into the habit of doing it.

There are a few rules when it comes to identifiers. First, they can contain underscores and alphanumeric characters, but must always start with a letter and are case sensitive. It's also possible to put spaces in your identifier, but if you do this, you'll need to wrap the name in backquotes (or back tics, depending on your preference) for example (`this has a space`). For simple queries it makes sense to use an easy identifier so in a lot of cases something as simple as `(n)` will be more than adequate.

With that note about identifiers out of the way it's time to move on. As mentioned earlier, when you create nodes, it's possible to add labels to them to make finding them easier later on. In most cases you may use one label, but multiple labels can be used if it suits your data.

If you want to use a label in your query, then it can be done like so `(n:Person)`. In this case the label is `Person`, but still using `n` as the identifier. Now if you had a complex query that returned different types of nodes, you may want to use a more specific identifier so that it can be reused at a later point. Something like `(people:Person)` will allow us to use the keyword "`people`", instead of `n`, later on in our query. If additional labels are required, you can just add them like so: `(james:Person:Relative)`. In this case, the identifier for the node is `james` and there are two labels, `Person` and `Relative`.

In terms of just nodes by themselves, that pretty much covers the basic pattern. Of course, the node pattern can be used with properties, and the pattern is required when querying relationships, but these will be covered in their respective sections, so we may as well move on to properties.

Properties

A property is useless by itself, as they need to be applied to either a node, or a relationship, which is why Nodes came first. When it comes to representing properties, this is done using curly braces {} and in most cases a property will be inside the parentheses of a node. When performing a read-based query (getting data out of the database) then the property will act as a filter, whereas when creating or updating nodes, the properties will be set onto that node so depending on the context, properties can have multiple functions.

There are other times when properties are used, but the most common format they'll be seen in will be `(n:People {name: "Chris"})` and its function would be altered depending on the context of its use. In the case of `(n:People {name: "Chris"})` we are looking for all "People" nodes, `n`, with a name property of `"Chris"`, which we know is a string literal from the double quotes. Many different value types can be used when saving properties, which can be seen in Table 4-1, but the easiest type is a string, as if it's not a numeric value or an array, it's a string. The names for properties work in the same way the nodes, so they must start with a letter, be alphanumeric, and are case sensitive. Again like with nodes, if you want to use spaces you can, but these must be wrapped in backquotes, the "`" character, in order to work.

Table 4-1. *Different datatypes available within Neo4j*

Property type	Explanation
Numerical values	Essentially, you can store any numerical value you want. The limits of this come from the JVM, in particular the Long, Float and Double integer types, so if you have some bespoke use cases for numerical property values, look in that direction. Otherwise, Neo4j in most cases will be fine with whatever number you throw at it.
String	Strings are fine to use within Neo4j, and will be stored without any craziness.
Boolean	Booleans are stored as `true`/`false`, and are stored without any real issue, in lower case. If you create a node with say TRUE, it'll lower case the value when stored. You can however still write cypher queries using uppercase Boolean values, and it will still work the same way.
Array	You can store arrays in Neo4j, but arrays have certain rules. An array must contain values of the same type. An array of different types (A string, an int, and a Boolean, for example) isn't supported. If you tried to store an array of multiple types, cypher will cast all values in the array to whatever the type of the first item is, so a string, integer, and a Boolean would save as three strings, e.g., "string", "100", "true".

In addition, you cannot create a node with an empty array, because Neo4j needs to know the type when storing the array. Once the type has been determined, the array can then be emptied. If you had an array of strings (such as the example above) you could then empty that array, but any values added to it, would be cast as strings, because that's the array type, and the type doesn't change. |

Multiple properties can be specified when performing queries as needed. Each property identifier and value pair needs to be separated with a comma, just be sure not to leave a trailing one, or you'll get a Cypher query error. This comes in really handy when creating nodes with a lot of properties, or creating when you want to return a very specific subset of nodes.

It's not just nodes that can have properties added to them; relationships are also able to have them assigned, which makes being able to query nodes (or saving information about the relationship) really easy. Speaking of relationships, let's discuss them, shall we?

Relationships

Relationships are probably one of the most powerful features within Neo4j and graph databases in general, and Cypher makes them really easy to use, both in terms of creation and retrieval. For a relationship to happen, there needs to be things to relate, and what do you relate in Neo4j? Nodes.

Depending on whether or not you're querying a relationship, or creating one, the pattern of the relationship is slightly different. When creating a relationship, you need to at the very least specify a direction, so at the very basic level, nodes can be related like so:

```
(a)- ->(b)
```

This shows that `a` is related to `b`, which can be seen by the use of an arrow, as it's pointing to the node it's related to. This relationship has no type, or properties, or an identifier, though, so it's a very basic relationship. A more complex example of creating a relationship would be something like:

```
(j:Kerbal {name: "Jeb"})-[r:KNOWS]->(b:Kerbal {name: "Bill"})
```

The important part of the pattern is in the middle, as the first and last parts are just nodes. This particular pattern could be used to create a relationship between these nodes, or to search the database for nodes that met the correct criteria. The nodes here have the label of `Kerbal` with the property `name` with the value of Jeb, and another by the `name` of `Bill`.

In case the reference to `Kerbal` is lost on you never fear, as they're just the race of people used in the game Kerbal Space Program which is a brilliant game. The names Bill and Jeb are in the game, however they're the favorite characters of my favorite YouTuber, Robbaz. Not relevant to Neo4j, but always nice to know.

Anyway, that example has a bit more information than the basic one, as it's not just an arrow this time, there are also square brackets (or brackets, as they're actually called) in this one. Names aren't required if you don't need them, that's why the first example had none. So, with nothing to go in the brackets, they were removed. Inside the brackets you can give the relationship an identifier if you'd like to use it later in the query, and also a type. The types are similar to a nodes label, however you can only have one type per relationships, but you can have many relationships between nodes.

The `-[r:KNOWS]->` part of the query is what we're interested in. Here `r` is the identifier (which could be omitted if it's not needed), the type (all caps and underscores are allowed) and if they were needed, properties too. The head of the arrow is pointing right in this case, but can be on either side depending on the relationship, inwards or outwards.

In this example the relationship being created was that Jeb knows Bill, but not that Bill knows Jeb. Essentially this means, if you were to get every node with that relationship, then only Jeb knowing Bill would be returned, not the other way around. In cases where relationships work both ways, the relationship was just created twice, with the direction of the relationship flipped in the second query.

This just means that you're able to create one-way relationships that can be inward or outward. Another example would be say, a dog and its owner. If there were Dog nodes and Person nodes, the Person could be related to the dog with an `OWNER` relationship, but this wouldn't work the other way around.

Of course, this has just covered a one-to-one relationship, what about a chain of relationships? This is entirely possible in Neo4j and is known as a Path, although all relationships are paths really, just of different lengths. Paths are what makes Neo4j exciting, and where a lot of its power lies. Cypher also gives control over how it queries Paths. This is covered as needed in the next part of the chapter.

Querying Cypher

Knowing the patterns to perform a query is great, but without knowing how to query Cypher in the first place, you aren't going to get very far. Depending on your use case, there are a number of ways to communicate with Cypher, which will be covered in a bit more detail momentarily. By far the most universal way is to use the REST API via HTTP, which will work regardless of your system. In these examples I'll be using `curl` to interact with the API, as it's the most common way of doing so. Before the `curl` side of things, let's go through the easier way using the brilliant Neo4j Browser.

Browser

By far the easiest way to query your database with Cypher is by using the browser. Depending on what stage you're up to in terms of development, how you use the Browser will be different, however it always has uses. Whether this is for adding nodes, reviewing data, or performing certain admin actions.

In the early stages, it helps when getting used to the syntax of Cypher, gives useful error messages, keeps a history of your previous queries, shows you your results, and many more things. Even after the inlaid stages, the Browser is brilliant for debugging your application, so if you're getting a strange return from Neo4j, checking the Cypher query in the Browser can help to work out if it's the query that's wrong, or if the issues lie somewhere else. You can of course get a query working as needed in the Browser and then use in your application after it works as expected, which makes things a lot easier.

The Browser was created to allow interaction with the data within the database, so of course the prompt to perform Cypher queries is at the top of the page, with space below for the query history. To the right of the prompt are the options to save the query for later, create a new query, or execute the query.

The console also allows you to perform keyboard actions that you'd be used to in a proper editor, so highlighting words for copy/pasting is easy, and as an added bonus, pressing return will run the query, just like a proper terminal, so the experience of using it is very nice.

For every query performed (even the ones with errors) it adds another item below the prompt, so you have a full query history available at all times, which is really useful. Each item also comes with options to either Export the resulting data, delete the item from the history, or make that particular result set full screen, which can be seen when you hover over an item. The fullscreen view is excellent for navigating a large result graph, or if you happen to return a large amount of properties and having the additional ROM is rather beneficial.

Although it's possible to query data easily in the Browser, it can also be used to update or create nodes, relationships, and also manage the properties for these. It's a very nice interface to interact with Cypher, and thanks to the query history and the instant feedback on errors, it's a very powerful tool.

If you find yourself performing the same queries often, it may be worth saving the query for later use, as mentioned earlier. If you save a query, it'll be available for later use via the 'Saved queries` button on the left of the Browser, which happens to be a star to keep things easy. When the save button is pressed, it'll open up the saved scripts dialog for you regardless, and if you have a query in the prompt when it is pressed, that query will be added to the list. The star will also highlight to show the query has been saved.

After you save a query, changes can be made to it quite easily, so if the query changes, you can just select it from the saved scripts menu, which will load it into the prompt, ready to execute. If any changes are made, the star will change to an exclamation mark to show changes have been made, so just hit this button when you're finished with the modifications, and it'll be updated. You can of course just run the query and it won't be updated.

Using the Browser is the easiest way to interact with your data, but is of course useless in applications, so when it comes to it being used in an application, it needs to use the REST API (which the Browser uses under the hood anyway) so let's move from the Browser to that, shall we?

REST API

You communicate to Neo4j using its REST API, which allows you to manage your database by using certain endpoints, headers, and sending certain data to these endpoints. Through using these things in different combination you can do anything we've mentioned, creating nodes, and relationships, but without using Cypher. In previous version of Neo4j, Cypher had its own dedicated endpoint to use, so you would essentially send your Cypher query to `http://localhost:7474/db/data/cypher` and get a response back. This of course assumes you have Neo4j set up using the default path and ports. The usage of the REST API directly to perform Cypher queries may be overkill for most cases, but it's still good to cover how it's possible. In the new version, there is still an endpoint available to run Cypher queries, but it's now done via the transaction endpoint.

We've touched on transactions before, but just in case it's escaping your mind, a database transaction is a group of queries bundled together, so that it's possible to roll back the previous actions if one fails, for example. For the most part that doesn't matter though as the queries will be one-offs in the examples, so the transaction will only have one action inside of it.

To get back on track, as previously mentioned `curl` will be used to interact with Neo4j at these examples. One thing that needs to be added to the curl command is an authentication header, which is now required so you'll need your Neo4j username and password to interact with the database via curl.

In previous versions of Neo4j, the authentication module was disabled, so unless you wanted it to be secured, Neo4j would be open, so no username and password would be required. Now though, as of version 2.2 Neo4j requires authentication, which is why you need to login to the Browser on first use. In addition to logging in, you need to change your password on first use, which is another security measure, but after all of these processes are complete, there will be a set of credentials that you have, which give you access to Neo4j. If you tried to communicate with Neo4j without changing the password, you would get an authentication error, telling you that you need to change your password. The easiest way to get around this problem is to log in via the browser and change your password when prompted to do so. For the sake of ease, I'll use the default values for these, which is a username of `neo4j` and also a password `neo4j` but your password will be different, as you need to change it on first use, as previously mentioned.

We already know the endpoint we'll be interacting with, which is the transaction endpoint, as it's the only way to perform Cypher queries using the REST API. The endpoint being used is `http://localhost:7474/db/data/transaction/commit` (again, assuming the defaults are used) which you would also use if you were to perform a transaction with the API also, but we're using it for Cypher queries. This endpoint is a little different, as it's essentially for transactions that have one action. You'll use the `commit` segment in the URL, which is essentially committing this transaction immediately, making it like a normal query, so we'll be using this endpoint for our Cypher queries.

To perform the query, the basic version of the curl command is as follows:

```
curl -i -H "Content-Type: application/json" -X POST -u neo4j:neo4j http://localhost:7474/db/
data/transaction/commit
```

There are many ways to perform curl queries, whether it's in a Terminal window (Mac and Linux, that is, the Windows command prompt doesn't support curl by default) or by installing one of the many available chrome extensions, or desktop applications. One popular Chrome extension is called Postman, but there are many other options.

The query in this case (which will be explained in more detail below) is a POST request, so it can also be done using any technology capable of sending a POST request. Although the examples will be done in curl, if you're more comfortable using another platform to perform these queries, then by all means do so. A breakdown of the query params can be seen Table 4-2.

Table 4-2. *Query Parameters*

Flag	Explanation
-i	This adds an HTTP header to the response, and in this case is optional. The header can be useful to help debug issues, but if it's not supplied, then only the response from the server is shown and nothing else, which in this case will be JSON.
-H	This is the header flag, and allows you to add content headers to the request. In this case, we're telling the server that the content we're sending over is JSON. This is important, as the server expects JSON, so if it's not in the correct format, it won't do anything.
-X	Represents the request type, which can be typically POST, DELETE, PUT, and the default GET. In essence we're posting to the endpoint and getting a result, so it's just like a remote form.
-u	Finally the authentication for the request. If you didn't have this, it would give an authentication error, and also if these details were wrong.
-d	This is the data sent along with the request, if it's needed. This can be POST variables, or even a string of JSON, which is what we'll be using it for.
-v (optional)	When you're debugging (or learning, in this case) it's generally to get as much information as possible to help find the solution. With curl requests, this comes in the form of the verbose flag, which when used essentially gets curl to explain itself, and the steps the command is taking are output to the screen.
	You may not want that additional information to be displayed (which is why I've marked it as optional) as it outputs a lot more information, but depending on the use case it can be useful. To use the flag, just add it like the other flags, just be sure not put it between the flag and its argument, such as after -X, because -X expects the type to follow it, for example.

If this query were to be run now, it wouldn't do anything, as no data is being sent over, which is why the `-d` flag is needed, which is where the JSON (including the Cypher query) is sent. Before the full query is used, let's have a look at the JSON:

```
{
    "statements" : [
        { "statement" : "MATCH (n) RETURN n;" }
    ]
}
```

A query is described as a statement when submitting to the transaction endpoint, so essentially the JSON above is an array of 'statements', with one 'statement' inside it. Although the transactions in this case are only one statement, if you were to add multiple statements it would look something like the following:

```
{
    "statements" : [
        { "statement" : "MATCH (n:Person) RETURN n;" },
        { "statement" : "MATCH (n:Pet) RETURN n;" }
    ]
}
```

37

You'll notice `n` is used in both queries which would cause an error if it was in the same query, but since these queries are performed in isolation from each other (although still grouped within the same transaction) then using the same alias isn't an issue.

To make the queries in the chapter easier to read, they've been spread over multiple lines, but when you're running queries on the command line it's generally easier to remove the formatting and run everything on a single line. Below is an example of the curl query from earlier with the JSON required to perform the query, so pretty much everything is in one command.

curl -i -H "Content-Type: application/json" -X POST -u neo4j:password http://localhost:7474/db/data/transaction/commit -d '{"statements" : [{ "statement" : "MATCH (n) RETURN n;" }]}'

With all components of the query in place, if the query is run now, it'll return every node with all of the properties attached to them, which depending on the structure of your nodes, will look something like:

```
{
    "results": [{
        "columns": ["n"],
        "data": [{
            "row": [{
                "uid": "1",
                "date": "29-03-15",
                "value": "10",
                "stat_id": "3"
            }]
        }, {
            "row": [{
                "uid": "1",
                "date": "24-04-15",
                "value": "1",
                "stat_id": "4"
            }]
        }]
    }],
    "errors": []
}
```

The JSON returned consists of two arrays, 'results' and 'errors'. In this case, there is only one item in the result array, because only one statement has been run, but multiple statements would result in multiple result sets. Within the result set, the columns are whatever you have returned, so in this case it is `n` which is what I specified in the return statement. Each row with the results is a node, and each item within a row is the properties of the node being returned. One thing you may notice here is the lack of node ids, which is because they need to be returned in a certain way, which will be covered a little later on. If you had returned a relationship instead of a node, then each item within the results would be a relationship.

The JSON returned here can be used within an application however it's needed, so whether you have one or many sets of results, they can be iterated over without any real issue, In this instance the errors array is empty (because there aren't any, of course) but if there were any errors, then they would be output within the errors array, so if it's empty, there have been no errors.

Although this was a read query, write queries work in the same way so using this method of performing Cypher queries via curl, you can manage all of your Neo4j actions from the command line, if you'd like to. To make this process a little easier though, developers have created a number of libraries to interact with Neo4j, so rather than having to write the query yourself you can just use a function, method, or whatever the developer has deemed appropriate. There are many different options available for multiple programming languages, so if you'd like to use a library, you'll most likely find one.

How to Build a Cypher Query

With the basics covered, it's time to cover the anatomy of the queries, and show what the different keywords and functions that can be used are, and also how they work. When covering the syntax, I made a point of leaving out keywords to ensure the usage in each context could be covered separately, without duplication. Each item will have an example with it, so seeing how it gets used is as easy as possible. Plus, this has the added bonus of being a great reference guide when you think to yourself "Ah, I know I can do that, but I can't remember how" and with a quick glance it'll all come flooding back.

A Quick note on Comments

Before we dive into the anatomy of Cypher queries, it's worth mentioning comments. A comment, is a string of text that can be used within the query, but isn't executed. You initiate a comment by starting the string with `//` which makes the text following it a comment, and because of that, not executed. You can include a comment on a new line in a query, or at the end of a particular part, an example can be seen below:

```
MATCH (n) RETURN n; //Return all of the nodes, on one line
```

The text within the comment isn't executed. The same goes for between lines, as well, like so:

```
MATCH (n)
//Time to return some nodes
RETURN n
```

The only time a comment won't act like a comment is when it's within quotes, as it then becomes a string, for assigning to a property, for example.

Enough on that though, it's time to get started, starting with a clause you'll see a lot, RETURN.

RETURN

If you want to use the data you're referencing in a query, then it'll need to be returned; otherwise, the query will just execute and you won't get anything back. This is fine for creating nodes or relationships as you don't always want what you've just created to be returned, but when it comes to querying data, you'll want it returned, or at least part of it.

There's been a lot of talk of aliases, and the main use for an alias is when it's being returned, or of course if you're using it later in the query. If you reference a node with `n`, then you can use `RETURN n` to have access to that node's data within your code. The same applies to relationships. You won't always want the full node, what if you only want the `name` property value from your node? That's not a problem, in this case `n.name` would just be used after the return. You can also return multiple properties by comma separating them, like so: `RETURN n.name, n.age`. This can also be achieved with multiple nodes, so if you're referencing a relationship, you may have node `a` and node `b`, you can return properties from a, and b, or both nodes, or nothing. It all depends on your needs. There is always the option of using `*` as well, which will return everything.

When it comes to return, essentially just think about what you need to use in your application, if you realize you only use certain properties, then just return those properties. If you have a lot of complex nodes, returning single properties will optimize the query and make it faster. There's also the added bonus of optional properties, so even if the value is null for that node it won't error, it'll just return null. Although the speed increase is small as Neo4j is already pretty fast, any speed increase is better than nothing, right?

If you need a return value to have a certain name to make your code easier, you can just alias the query by using `AS` so an example would be `RETURN n AS Person` so accessing the returned data in code would be much easier. You can also return unique results, just in case your query would return multiple ones. You can do this by adding `DISTINCT` to your query.

There's also the option to perform last-minute filters on results. If you have a numeric value, or any other that can be evaluated against, you can use something like `RETURN n.age > 30` which will only return nodes with an age over 30, easy!

If you're returning a node, you can also return its relationships if you want to. Since you can use commas to add an argument to a return clause, if you want the nodes relationships you can just add it to the clause. To do this, just use `(n)-->()` which assuming your node is aliased with `n`, it'll add the nodes relationships to the response.

MATCH

When writing Cypher queries, you'll no doubt see MATCH a lot, as it's the main way to query the data and potentially return results. Using match allows you to get information on nodes, properties, and relationships, but filtering them using various clauses. Let's quickly run through some of the basic query patterns you may see.

```
MATCH (n)
RETURN n;
```

This will return any nodes stored within the database.

```
MATCH (n:Person { name: "Chris" })
RETURN n;
```

This will match any nodes that have the label `Person`, the property `name`, and the value of said property is `Chris`.

```
MATCH (a)--(b)
RETURN a, b;
```

Here we're matching nodes that are related, regardless of the direction (notice the lack of an arrow) and returning the nodes from both sides.

```
MATCH (a)-[r]-(b)
RETURN a, r, b;
```

In this case, the relationships have been assigned to the `r` variable, which means they can be returned from the query, so if you need the relationship (or any of its properties) then it can be returned easily enough.

```
MATCH (a)-[:RELATED]->(b)
RETURN a, b;
```

When you don't want to wildcard everything, you may want to have a certain type of relationship, which is added with the `:TYPE` pattern. In this case, the type is RELATED and since the relationship isn't needed later the alias has been dropped.

Rather than only returning the nodes involved in a path, you may want the path itself, which can also be done easily enough. Using the previous example, that'll be made into a named path.

```
MATCH p=(a)-[:RELATED]->(b)
RETURN p;
```

It's possible to use multiple MATCH clauses in a query so if you wanted to return two particular nodes, you could just use multiple match causes and then return the result, like so:

```
MATCH (a:Person {name: 'Chris'})
MATCH (b:Person {name: 'Kane'})
RETURN a, b;
The previous query could also be rewritten as follows and would still give the same result,
using one MATCH.
MATCH (a:Person {name: 'Chris'}),(b:Person {name: 'Kane'})
RETURN a, b;
```

This would return the nodes requested just as you would expect, if the nodes can be found. If the second MATCH failed, then the first one would also fail, and the query would return 0 results, as it's looking for a AND also b, in this case, therefore if it can't find `b` then the query isn't valid. You can get around this though, by using an optional match. This will essentially return the match if it's there, if not it'll return `null`, so the query still works.

```
MATCH (a:Person {name: 'Chris'})
OPTIONAL MATCH (b:Person {name: 'Kane'})
RETURN a, b;
```

You can also use the optional flag to return potential relationships for a node. If the node only might have a relationship, then an optional flag can be used to remedy this, like so:

```
MATCH (a:Person {name: 'Chris'})
OPTIONAL MATCH (a)-->(x)
RETURN a, x;
```

For all of the `Person` labeled nodes with the `name` of `Chris` both the nodes that do and don't have relationships will be returned.

You may also see uses of `START` in some example queries online. Match now is what start used to be, but now it's depreciated and is only used if you want to pick out something from a legacy index. Going forward though, you shouldn't see or use start in your queries anyway with it being depreciated, but if you see `START` anywhere, at least the knowledge on it is there.

CREATE/CREATE UNIQUE

This clause is one you'll be familiar with, as we've covered it briefly before, but CREATE does what it says, creates things. This can be a node, a relationship, a node with a relationship, a node with properties, or any combination of these. One good thing about return queries, is that you don't always have to return anything.

If you're just creating a new node or relationship, then there isn't anything to return, which will make your query smaller. Of course the option to return from the query is there, but it's not required. A create can be as simple as `CREATE (n)` which would create a node with no label, or properties.

```
CREATE (n:Person:Developer)
Here we can see an example with multiple labels, but no properties.
CREATE (n:Person { name : 'Chris', job_title : 'Developer' })
This example has multiple properties on a node which also has a label.
MATCH (a:Person),(b:Person)
WHERE a.name = 'Chris' AND b.name = 'Kane'
CREATE (a)-[r:RELATED {relation: "brother"}]->(b)
RETURN r
```

In this example two previously created nodes are being matched, using MATCH and WHERE, and then CREATE is used to add the relationship between the previously matched nodes. In this case, there's a RELATED relationship being added here, with a property of 'relation: brother' to give some context to the relationship.

You can already create relationships with newly created nodes too, so the following example would create two nodes, and a relationship:

```
CREATE (:Person {name: "Bill"})-[:KNOWS]->(:Person {name: "Bob"})
```

If you ran this query again however, it would create duplicate nodes, which isn't always ideal. Duplicates can be reduced with query constraints, but depending on the use case, this isn't always needed.

Being able to create a unique Node or Relationship can come in very useful, for duplication reduction, and also updating existing nodes. To achieve this, you can use CREATE UNIQUE, which essentially performs a MATCH without you having to. Using CREATE UNIQUE means if you're say, adding a relationship to a Node, you can safely use a create query without the worry of duplication. An example of that would be:

```
MATCH (bill:Person {name: "Bill"})
CREATE UNIQUE (bill)-[r:KNOWS]->(bob:Person {name: "Bob"})
RETURN r
```

In this case, if the `Bob` node didn't exist, it would be created, with the relationship. If the query was run again though, then the "Bob" node wouldn't be duplicated, and neither would the relationship. This means you can have some control over duplication of data within your applications.

DELETE/REMOVE

There always comes a time when you need to delete data, whether it's a user that has left, or a comment that's been deleted, there's always a need, and that's what DELETE does. This clause is very simple to use, and is used to delete Nodes, and Relationships. When deleting nodes you must remember that if you delete it, unless you delete its relationships as well, it will remain. A basic usage of DELETE is as easy as:

```
MATCH (n:RemoveMe)
DELETE n
```

In the query, DELETE essentially takes the place of RETURN and deletes whatever is matched in the query, which in this case is any nodes with the label `RemoveMe`. This label could have been added by a worker and flagged for deletion with the `RemoveMe` label.

When it comes to removing the relationships it can be done in one step, just use MATCH to get the Relationships and delete them, which can be done using:

```
MATCH (n:RemoveMe)-[r]-()
DELETE n, r
```

The main change here is the inclusion of `r` which is the alias of the relationships (either direction) found with MATCH. There comes a time when you may be working on a project and need to clear out your database frequently. This snippet can be used to remove relatively small amounts of data easily to allow you to start again. The snippet in question is:

```
MATCH (n)
OPTIONAL MATCH (n)-[r]-()
DELETE n,r
```

This isn't recommended for large datasets, as it will attempt to delete all the nodes and relationships at once, which will be quite intensive. For deleting larger amounts of data, it's possible to use DELETE with LIMIT, allowing for batches to be utilized. LIMIT will be covered in more detail later in the chapter.

You don't always want to remove the entire node though; just certain Properties or Labels, which can be achieved using REMOVE. The main concept for REMOVE is the same as DELETE, you use MATCH to get the nodes you wish to modify, then do so with REMOVE, which looks like this:

```
MATCH (bill { name: 'Bill' })
REMOVE bill.subscription_start
RETURN bill
```

This example would be used if Bill had decided he didn't want the newsletter anymore, so code in the application needed his `subscription_start` property to be removed. Labels work in the same way, just MATCH it, then REMOVE it, like so:

```
MATCH (n { name: 'Sara' })
REMOVE n:Remove
RETURN n
```

In this scenario it's assumed that there is only one node with the Property 'Sara', and that said node already has a `Remove` label.

WHERE

The WHERE clause is a powerful one as it allows you to filter your queries, to get more specific results. Although WHERE is powerful, it's useless without `MATCH`, `OPTIONAL MATCH`, `START`, or `WITH`, as it needs something to feed it data to filter.

So WHERE is a filter, but one with a lot of flexibility and power, and if you're from an SQL background, you'll be familiar with this already, as the behavior is essentially the same.

Being able to filter on if a node has a certain relationship, if a property matches a pattern, or as little as a property equals a value; this is just a taste of WHERE's power, but enough talk, let's get into some examples starting simple then getting more complex.

```
MATCH (n:Developer)
WHERE n.name = 'Chris'
RETURN n;
```

This example would only return nodes with the label `Developer`, with the property of `name`, and a value of `Chris`.

You can also use WHERE to filter based on value ranges using `<` and `>` such as `WHERE n.age > 30` which would mate any nodes with the property `age` with a value of greater than 30.

```
MATCH (n:Developer)
WHERE n.age > 30
RETURN n;
```

You can also combine WHERE with AND, OR, and NOT to build up some really specific results. Let's have a look at an example:

```
MATCH (n:Person)
WHERE n.age > 18 AND (n.name = 'Chris' OR n.name = "Kane") AND (n)-[:RELATED {relation:
"brother"}]-()
RETURN n;
```

This was a big example, but let's go over it in chunks. The first part of WHERE is the filter on if `n.age` is greater than 18, followed by AND, which is checking if `name` is `Chris` or `Kane` enclosed in brackets to ensure the `AND` is used properly. Next up is checking to make sure the node has the `RELATED` relationship, and the relationship property is equal to `brother`. This is why no direction is specified when checking the relationship, and that empty parentheses are used rather than a node directly.

This is a very specific way of getting me and my brother, or anybody else who happens to be called Chris and Kane and are also brothers. Depending on the dataset this would be a bit much, so if you had a smaller dataset, the extra constraint on the relationship may not have been needed.

If you need to ensure a property exists on the nodes you return, then EXISTS is here to help.

```
MATCH (n:Developer)
WHERE EXISTS(n.subscription_start)
RETURN n;
```

In this instance, the nodes in question have started a subscription to something and the date has been stored, so if they're sending out a newsletter, those that haven't subscribed won't be bothered. The EXISTS function can also be used for relationships, as well as nodes.

When working with property values, sometimes you may want nodes with a certain value, or even those that don't have a property set. When a property isn't set on a node, it'll return NULL, so if you're expecting a value to not be there, you must address it directly, which looks like this:

```
MATCH (n)
WHERE n.level = 'beginner' OR n.level IS NULL
RETURN n
ORDER BY n.name
```

This would get all those that were `n.level` as 'beginner' or if the level hadn't been set, and was NULL.

It's also possible to utilize Regular expressions, within your queries. You can declare a pattern by using `=~` followed by the pattern. An example of this would be:

```
MATCH (n)
WHERE n.name =~ '(?i)^[a-d].*'
RETURN n
```

The use of `(?i)` in the expression makes the whole thing case insensitive, that's why that's there. This particular example gets any names that start with the letters between `a` and `d`. This would only really be used if you had a huge amount of people in a list, and were batching e-mails to send out, or something of that nature.

You can also essentially inverse a query to exclude those particular nodes by using `NOT`. One usage would be:

```
MATCH (n)
WHERE NOT n.name = 'Chris'
RETURN n
```

This would give every other node that wasn't `name` equals `Chris`. Maybe somebody needs to send an e-mail about planning my birthday party or something, who knows? That silliness aside, `NOT` can be very useful in complex queries when you have a tricky filter and certain values keep creeping in: "Uck, yes, them, but not you guys!".

ORDER BY

This clause pretty much does what it says on the tin, it allows you to order the data by something, more specifically, properties. This can be useful if you want to alphabetize a list, order people by age, or anything like that. You can sort a response by the properties on a node or relationship, but not by the nodes or relationships themselves. A basic example is something like:

```
MATCH (n)
RETURN n
ORDER BY n.name
```

You'll notice that the `ORDER BY` is after the RETURN, which is required, and will result in an error if it's not in the correct place. Although ordering by one property is good, it's also possible to sort by multiple values, which can be achieved by adding a comma, like so:

```
MATCH (n)
RETURN n
ORDER BY n.age, n.name
```

When it comes to sorting null values, these will appear at the end of the list, so most importantly, it doesn't break the query if the value isn't there. By default the sort order is ascending, so if you'd like a descending order, just add `DESC` at the end of the query, which will reverse the order, this also means that if you do have null values, they'll be at the start, rather than the end of the query. The previous example, reversed, would be:

```
MATCH (n)
RETURN n
ORDER BY n.age DESC, n.name DESC
```

In this case I've reversed both properties, but it only needs to be added to the applicable property.

INDEXES

Using indexes is always recommended, but isn't always possible. An index is a redundant copy of the information that's being indexed, to make looking up said information faster. When they can be used, indexes make things faster, and that's always good, but it's possible to have too much of a good thing. Storing an index takes up space, and also lowers write speed. This comes from the indexes needing to be updated when new information is stored in the database, creating a performance cost.

Neo4j allows you to create an index on properties of nodes that share the same label. If there is a particular property that you happen to query a lot, then it may be worth adding an index for it, if it doesn't already have one. In some cases an index can be automatically assigned, such as constraints, which will be covered in a moment. It's also possible to have a nodes property sit in multi indexes, which has the potential to cause problems. In the cases of multiple indexes, then the USING clause can be utilized, allowing you to specify which index the query will use. Unless USING is specified, Cypher will work out what it believes to be the most logical index to use if some are there to use, and will do this without any additional input from the user. We'll also cover USING a little later.

If you create an index in Neo4j it'll be automatically updated. This includes any updates to node that have properties in an index and also when new nodes are created meeting the required criteria. Adding an index can be as easy as:

```
CREATE INDEX ON :Person(name)
```

This creates an index on any nodes with a `Person` Label and a name property, and will also be used automatically, as soon as it is ready. When the query to create an index is received by Neo4j, it's not added immediately, and will be used internally as soon as it is ready. This is for performance reasons, and the index is created in the background to keep everything fast (adding an index on a huge dataset may take some time, because creating an index is blocking, and atomic) but once it's done it'll be used automatically.

As mentioned earlier, you can sometimes have too many indexes, which can actually hinder performance. It may also be that you have a particularly large index that doesn't get used too often, and you want to save space by removing it. If you decide you don't want a particular index anymore, that's fine, it can be dropped as easily as it was created by using:

```
DROP INDEX ON :Person(name)
```

This will drop the index, and the database will act as though it never existed. If you change your mind you can always create the index again.

CONSTRAINTS

Using constraints helps keep your data unique, and its integrity intact. Data integrity can mean different things to different people, but for a registration-based system, having duplicates would be classified as an integrity violation. Unique constraints are extremely useful when working with information like e-mail addresses or usernames that are required to be unique, and can cause issues if they aren't.

When a constraint is created, it creates an index for the properties that are required to be unique. This is used to help keep track of the existing values, so if it's not in the index, then its unique value. When the constraint is created, the index is also, so no need to manually create the index. Once the index has been built and all nodes scanned, then it is available, and used on queries thereafter. If you have data within the database that violates the unique constraint, then said constraint will fail to be created. In the event that a constraint fails to be applied to your graph, you need to resolve any redundancy issues with your data before attempting to apply the constraint again. For this reason, it's advisable that you add your constraints sooner rather than later to avoid this type of clean-up. In most cases though, you'll just create a constraint, and then that'll be it, which can be as easy as:

```
CREATE CONSTRAINT ON (p:Person) ASSERT p.email IS UNIQUE
```

As with an index, a constraint is added on nodes with a certain label and property combination. In this case `Person` and `email` respectively. If you try and create a node that violates the constraint, then the CREATE will produce an error and the node will not be created.

Just like indexes, constraints can be dropped, which is as easy as creating one in the first place, and looks like:

```
DROP CONSTRAINT ON (p:Person) ASSERT p.email IS UNIQUE
```

This would also remove the index used with the constraint, so if that index was helping with performance, or something of that nature, then it may be worth adding it back in after dropping the constraint, but in most cases it can be removed and then forgotten.

LIMIT

This clause simply limits the number of rows that'll be returned. Without the use of this clause, any applicable rows will be returned, which isn't always the desired outcome. There are many use cases for LIIMIT, from getting the first five registered users, to being able to list the top ten products within a system. Although both of these things could work well as a full list, sometimes you just want a small subset of data.

Being able to limit results is also useful when it comes to batch deleting items, or if you need to limit a result set to pass it on to another part of the query.

When using a limit, if the rows returned are greater than the limit when the limit is reached, no additional rows will be returned. This of course means if there are only 5 applicable rows when a LIMIT of 10 is specified, all 5 rows will be returned. It can be added to a query like so:

```
MATCH (n)
RETURN n
ORDER BY n.name
LIMIT 3
```

When using LIMIT, ensure it comes at the end of the query it's related to, as that's where it goes. In this example LIMIT is used to restrict the query to 3, so if there were 5 results, only 3 would be returned, but if there were only 2, then 2 would be returned.

SKIP

The `SKIP` clause works like an offset, so you essentially tell Cypher to skip the first x results. Using SKIP, in combination with LIMIT, allows things such as pagination to be created. In that case, your SKIP value would be the current page (+1 to avoid page 0) multiplied by the limit. Another potential use would be with promoted items. If there was a featured product on an e-commerce website, then the rest of the products were in a list, you'd want to SKIP 1 on the list query to avoid the featured product appearing. That is of course based on a number of assumptions, but the use case is sound.

If you wanted to skip the first row returned, then that can be as simple as:

```
MATCH (n)
RETURN n
ORDER BY n.name
SKIP 1
```

You can also combine SKIP and LIMIT together, so you can then limit the remaining rows down to a specified value. To build on the previous example, if we did only want the first 10 applicable rows after the first skipped one, it would look like so:

```
MATCH (n)
RETURN n
ORDER BY n.name
SKIP 1
LIMIT 10
```

WITH

The WITH clause is one that may be familiar to the Terminal savvy, as it's essentially a unix pipe. Essentially, WITH passes information to the next part of the query, but it can be used in different ways to achieve different goals. It can be used to filter down results, and make queries more efficient by stripping out unneeded data. It can also be used to collect additional data from a query, so it can be quite useful. Let's start with a filter, shall we?

```
MATCH (me { name: "Chris" })--(friend)-->()
WITH friend, count(*) AS foaf
WHERE foaf > 1
RETURN friend
```

In this example, the query is matching `me` then any connections I have to another node, aliased by `friend`. The query then looks for an outgoing relationship, so we're looking for a friend of a friend (hence foaf) here. The WITH is first of all passing the `friend` value, then is passing through a count of *, aliased with `foaf`. The `friend` value is required, otherwise the value couldn't be returned. In this example if you tried to return `me` the query would fail, as it's not passed onto the next stage of the query with WITH. The count is the sum of the friends my friend(s) have, as it's the last part in the path. The count is then used in the WHERE to ensure only my friends that know one other person are returned.

A common use of WITH is to order your data before you return it which can be pretty useful, but there's a bit more to it than that.

```
MATCH (me { name: "Chris" })--(f)
WITH f
ORDER BY f.name DESC
LIMIT 1
MATCH (f)--(fof)
RETURN fof.name
```

Since the MATCH has been aggregated with the WITH clause, it allows you to order the data before it's returned, and then limit that result, and then use it again straight away. Here the query is getting the related nodes of the matched one, after they have been sorted by the `name` property, in descending order, and limiting them to one. This query is essentially working out which of my friends has the name closest to the end of the alphabet, finding their friends, `fof`, and returning their names.

Next up is being able to aggravate data so that it can be collected, and also returned. So for the times you'd be looping through rows and collecting certain pieces of data, such as names, then this saves you the loop.

```
MATCH (n)
WITH n
ORDER BY n.name DESC LIMIT 3
RETURN collect(n.name)
```

The WITH aggregates the nodes so they can be ordered, and collected.

UNWIND

There may be times when you're querying data, where you have a collection, and you want to have rows. Well, that is just what UNWIND does, it takes collections of nodes, or arrays of data and splits them into individual rows again. When using UNWIND, the data must be aliased for the query to work. A very simple example is as follows:

```
UNWIND [ 'Chris', 'Kyle', 'Andy', 'Dave', 'Kane'] AS x
RETURN x
```

This would return all of the names in individual rows, rather than as a collection as they were passed in. You can also pass in structured data which can be iterated over within a query, and then used in combination with other clauses to make multiple changes, or you can even create nodes, too.

Using UNWIND in conjunction with MERGE (which we'll get to soon) can lead to a very efficient query that can create and/or update nodes and relationships. This situation implied that structured data has been passed into it, allowing it to be used by Cypher. An example of the data being passed in would be:

```
{
  "events" : [ {
    "year" : 2014,
    "id" : 1
  }, {
    "year" : 2014,
    "id" : 2
  } ]
}
```

This data can then be passed through to UNWIND and then, each item within the array of data can be passed through to something like MERGE, or even a CREATE statement. This means that rather than doing many creates, you can pass through data in an array, and make a query to do all of the hard work that only has to be done once. This doesn't mean to say you can't use a transaction and run a lot of queries that way, it's just another option.

UNION

This clause is used to return multiple queries, as if they were one, uniting them if you will. This can save you running multiple single queries, or to clean up the return statement of a more complex query. Say you had Tutor nodes and Pupil nodes, but just wanted names from both, UNION would be great there. If you were to return these in a normal statement you would need to return these values, probably aliased with two different things, such as `pupil_name` and `tutor_name` but with UNION, that's not a problem, and on using this example, the query would look like so:

```
MATCH (n:Tutor)
RETURN n.name
UNION ALL MATCH (n:Pupil)
RETURN n.name
```

This would return the results from both queries in one result set, so in this case it would be an array of names. In this example both of the property names were the same, but this isn't always the case, and doesn't need to be to take advantage of UNION. As long as the values are returned with the same names, then it doesn't matter if the name is the original property name, or an alias. An example of this can be seen as follows:

```
MATCH (n:Tutor)
RETURN n.tutor_name AS name
UNION ALL MATCH (n:Pupil)
RETURN n.pupil_name AS name
```

To use UNION you must first return everything you want from the first query, then add in UNION before performing the next query. You'll notice that in this example, `ALL` is present, which essentially returns the exact result from each query, maintaining duplicates. If you were to remove `ALL` then any duplicates within the result set would be removed, it's as easy as that.

It's worth noting you can also combine multiple `UNION`'s, but whatever they return must have the same name, so be sure to use an alias (`AS`) to ensure what you're returning from each query is consistently named with the others in the `UNION`.

USING

You'll only really need this clause if you're using a lot of indexes, because Neo4j takes care of which indexes to use automatically. There may be cases when Neo4j is using the wrong one and it's causing problems, so by using `USING` you specify an index to use for a particular query. An example of that would be as follows:

```
MATCH (n:Person)
USING INDEX n:Person(name)
WHERE n.name = 'Chris'
RETURN n;
```

In the example the `WHERE` clause is used to filter down a result set, and since there's already an index there, it can be selected with `USING`. Most of the time though, if you use indexes, then Neo4j will take care of a lot of the hard work for you. It's worth noting though that you can use multiple indexes in one query, so it can be manually controlled.

MERGE

Although its name suggests that MERGE will merge your data, that's not technically true. This clause ensures data exists within the graph, if it does the data will be merged and if not the data will be created. This sounds similar to how CREATE UNIQUE works, but MERGE is a lot more powerful.

When using MERGE, if all the properties in the query don't match a returned node, then a new node will be created. A basic example of MERGE works like so:

```
MERGE (bill { name:'Bill', age: 29 })
RETURN bill
```

Here, if there is a node with a `name` of `Bill` but there is no `age` set, then a new node would be created. The basic usage of MERGE is a mix of CREATE and MATCH, but there are some rules attached to this. The whole MERGE pattern matches, or it is created. This becomes even more important when using constraints, as this needs to return 1 node, or no nodes. If you were to perform a partial match, (such as multiple properties on the same node, as the same node would be returned for each property, which isn't unique) then the query will fail, so be careful with that. Constraints can be a hugely useful with MERGE, as it means you can create unique nodes, and if there's a problem, it'll error.

```
MERGE (char:Person { name:'Charlotte' })
RETURN char
```

If there was a constraint placed on the `name` property being unique (CREATE CONSTRAINT ON (n:Person) ASSERT n.name IS UNIQUE;) then this query would either match an existing node, or create a new one. You can also use the same logic on Relationships, using MERGE to create them as needed, to help once again with reducing duplicates within the code.

There is also a bit more control that can be gained by MERGE, with the use of ON CREATE and ON MATCH. Being able to use these clauses essentially gives the power to control the outcome of the query depending on if the query has MATCHed, or CREATEd a node, and you can use both in the same query too, which can be seen here:

```
MERGE (dave:Person { name:'Dave' })
ON CREATE SET dave.created = timestamp()
ON MATCH SET dave.last_login = timestamp()
RETURN dave
```

This example will SET (which will be covered, next actually) a "created" date for Dave if the node doesn't exist, otherwise the `last_login` property will be updated with a new value. Although in this example both "ON CREATE" and "ON MATCH" have been used, this isn't required and they can be used independently of each other, as well as together. The only thing to keep in mind is that the query used must be specific enough to return 1 or 0 nodes, because on a database with many people, the odds of having multiple people called "Dave" is most definitely a possibility. To improve the example, a unique identifier (such as an e-mail) could be used which would only ever return a single row (or none) provided the data was always kept unique, that is.

SET

The SET clause is used to update Labels on nodes, and also properties on Nodes and Relationships. To use SET you must first match the node you want to update, then just set the values you want to on said node, or relationship, depending on the use case. A basic example can be seen like so:

```
MATCH (n { name: 'Chris' })
SET n.username = 'chrisdkemper'
RETURN n
```

This would update the `Chris` node with the new username property, so if it didn't have the property before it'll be added, and if it did already exist it'll be updated. In this example the updated node was returned, but this isn't required and if it isn't needed, the RETURN can be omitted.

It's also possible to only add, and not update properties on a node, but using `+=` in the following way:

```
MATCH (n { name: 'Chris' })
SET n += { username: 'chrisdkemper' , level: 'admin'}
```

If the previous example was run first, then only the level part of this query would be respected, provided of course that the `level` property didn't already exist on the node. Multiple values can also be updated at once, they just need to be separated by a comma for properties, or by chaining multiple labels, like so:

```
MATCH (n { name: 'Chris' })
SET n.username = 'chrisdkemper' , n.level = 'admin'
```

This would update/set these properties depending on if they previously existed on the node or not. When dealing with Labels on Nodes, use the following:

```
MATCH (n { name: 'Chris' })
SET n :Moderator:Admin
RETURN n
```

This would set `Moderator` and `Admin` as labels for the matched node. It's also possible to remove a property by using SET, by setting a properties value to `NULL` which is essentially saying, you don't exist. There is a dedicated REMOVE clause for this, but it's still nice to know how it's possible with SET, which is achieved like so:

```
MATCH (n { name: 'Chris' })
SET n.level = NULL
RETURN n
```

By setting the `level` property value to NULL, it removes it from the node and would then need to be re-added to be used again.

shortestPath/allShortestPaths

After you've established a lot of data, or even if you haven't, you'll always end up wanting to find paths of some description, and there are functions in Cypher to achieve just that. If you don't have any/much data of your own the movie database is always available to you (which we covered in Chapter 2) from the browser. Anyway, say you have two people, you may want to how what the shortest path is between them. There could be a direct connection via a mutual friend, or one person's Grandma's, friend's, cousin may know the other person. Although that's farfetched (and made up) example, one of those paths is a lot shorter than the other. Using Cypher to work out the path can be achieved like so:

```
MATCH (bill:Person { name:"Bill" }),(bob:Person { name:"Bob" }),
p = shortestPath((bob)-[*..5]-(bill))
RETURN p
```

Using `shortestPath` here allows the path to be returned and used in an application. The same concept can also be applied to physical locations, where you can imagine a path as a route. An example of this would be train stations, so although the physical location wouldn't be taken into account (although this is possible, and will be discussed in Chapter 7), you can still see how far (or hops, as it is here) two stations are apart. In this case, however, inside the relationship square brackets it's specified that the relationship must be within 5 hops, so any responses here will be close ones.

If this query wasn't returning any results, it'd be possible to increase the maximum hops, or even remove the upper limit entirely, which would return the single shortest path regardless of length. When databases contain a lot of nodes, if possible it's advisable to add a limit to the number of hops the path will take.

If you'd then want to look at all the paths, then instead of `shortestPath` being used `allShortestPaths` is in its place. This works in the same way as `shortestPath` it just returns all paths, rather than just the shortest.

Key Functions

Neo4j has a lot of functions that can change how a query works, the return values, and many other things. For example, there are a number of mathematical functions that are used, which may be required if you're analyzing complex data, for example. If you're in a position that requires the use of a specific mathematical function within your query, than that information can be found easily enough online. There are however a number of functions that can be quite useful, so rather than detailing every function, a smaller collection of these useful functions will be mentioned instead.

count

There could be many reasons that values need to be counted in Cypher queries, and Neo4j has your back with the count function. Its use is easy enough, and essentially has two forms. The first form is just counting all of the resulting rows from the queries RETURN clause, which on a very basic level can be something like:

```
RETURN n, count(*)
```

In this instance, any nodes returned from the MATCH will be counted, and then added to the result set. The other use case for count is when you know what you want to count, and it has been aliased with something you can count, like so:

```
MATCH (n {name: "Chris"})-->(x)
RETURN count(x)
```

In this case, any nodes related to `Chris` will be counted, as they're aliased with `x` and that has been added to `count`. There is a chance that a query like this could have a lot of duplicates, which you can get around by using DISTINCT, so adding this to the previous example is as easy as:

```
MATCH (n { name: 'Chris' })-->(x)
RETURN count(DISTINCT x)
```

This means the count will only include unique values. Count can also be used to count non-null property values on nodes too, which is just as simple:

```
MATCH (n:Person)
RETURN count(n.subscription_start)
```

This will count how many of the labeled nodes have that property with an actual value, as it skips `null` values.

length

The length function is essentially like count, but for paths or collection, and returns a number value based on either the path hops, or the number of items within a collection. The function can take any collection as an argument (as paths are returned as collections) so just remember that when using it, or you will have a bad time. Enough chat, an example of `length` is:

```
MATCH p=(a)-->(b)
WHERE a.name='Chris'
RETURN length(p)
```

This query will return the length of every path returned (p) where the `Chris` node is related to any other node, so rather than the nodes themselves, the counts are returned. In more complex queries, length can be used to ensure paths are long enough, for instance, or just as an additional piece of data in a query.

type

In some queries, the type of a relationship doesn't matter, you just care that it exists, rather than what its type is. When the type does matter, and it needs to be explicitly returned, then that's where the `type` function comes in. It takes a relationship as an argument, then returns the type of the relationship supplied. An example of this is as follows:

```
MATCH (n)-[r]->()
WHERE n.name='Chris'
RETURN type(r)
```

This query will find any relationships that the `Chris` node has, and then return the type of the relationship, so the more relationships, the more rows returned.

id

This function can be very useful, as it returns the actual id for a node or relationship within the database. When a node is created it's assigned a numerical id, which cannot be set by a user. When a node is created, the previous node id is incremented and assigned to the new node. When a node is deleted, its ID then becomes available, so the next node created will get the newly available ID, rather than a new one. Relationships work in the same way, but rather than them both sharing the same set of IDs, nodes and relationships keep lists for this.

Although most of the querying in Cypher uses properties, sometimes you need the actual id, and the `id` function makes that easy. As with the other queries of its type, the node or relationship is first MATCH'ed and then passed into `id` where it is returned, which can look as simple as:

```
MATCH (n)
RETURN id(n)
```

This would return every node id in the database, as no query constraints have been added, but this would work in the same way, regardless of whether a WHERE or property filter was present. Speaking of WHERE, if you know a particular node's id and want to be able to query against it, then you need to select that node via a WHERE clause, like so:

```
MATCH (n)
WHERE id(n) = 150
RETURN n
```

For multiple IDs, an IN could also be used, if you knew the IDs of the nodes you wanted to return, that is.

timestamp

The timestamp function has a very simple task, return the milliseconds between now and January 1, 1970 UTC (Unix/POSIX Time timestamp). This is similar to how various other timestamp functions work in other programming languages. This can be useful if you want to say, check the servers timezone by running a simple:

```
RETURN timestamp()
```

Which would then return the timestamp in milliseconds for you to see. It can also be used when setting properly, so adding dynamic signup or creation, last sign in, and a number of other date-based operations can be simplified by using the `timestamp` function.

nodes/relationships

When you see a function called `nodes` or `relationships` you can assume (given the names) its use has something to do with nodes or relationships (depending on which one is used), and you'd be right. The `nodes` function is used to return the nodes within a supplied path, with the `relationships` function being used to return the relationships present in a path. Both functions require a path to be supplied as an argument in order for them to work. An example of the `node` function would be:

```
MATCH p=(a)-->(b)-->(c)
WHERE a.name='Chris' AND c.name='Kane'
RETURN nodes(p)
```

This will return all the nodes present in the path, but if `nodes` were to be replaced with `relationships` then instead of nodes, all the relationships present in the path would be returned.

labels

Although a lot of the time, nodes can be found using one label, what if you need all of the labels attached to a particular node? Well, that's what the `labels` function is for. This function takes a node as an argument, and returns an array of all the labels that are attached to it. An example of this would be:

```
MATCH (n)
WHERE n.name='Chris'
RETURN labels(n)
```

This would also work if more than one node were to be returned. A collection would be generated for each node being returned.

collect

This powerful little function allows the aggregation of data, so essentially makes many rows into one row, on a basic level. If you're getting one particular property from a node, then having to process each row, it may well be easier to get one row with every value inside it. That's what collect does, and it's very easy to use. A basic example would be:

```
MATCH (n:Person)
RETURN collect(n.name)
```

This query would return one row, with an array of the values of the `name` property on every `Person` node that has a name set. It also ignores null values, so that doesn't need to be considered either.

Summary

There's a lot of information in this chapter, but hopefully if it doesn't all go in on the first read, then this chapter will remain as a reference guide. We've gone from the very basics of building Cypher queries, to then making some complex and specific queries to ensure the data returned is as specific as possible. Of course this chapter doesn't contain everything, and as the book progresses more practical uses for the different Cypher query constraints will be unearthed, but the basic usage and explanation will be here.

■ ■ ■

CHAPTER 5

Managing Your Data in Neo4j

Thanks to it being a graph database, Neo4j actually gives you a lot of freedom when it comes to how you structure your data. When you're using something like MySQL, if you want to perform relationships, you have to adhere to certain rules. You'll need to have some kind of joining table for the data to join the different tables. Of course the way you structure the data is still similar in some respects, such as relating one node to another, but you don't need to use a table to do that; you could use a relationship, or a node and multiple relationships.

A quick note about Gists

In this chapter, we'll be covering some common pitfalls that can catch beginners, and then some example data structures that could be adapted for your own use. There's one issue with books that mention code in that sometimes, there are errors in the code, or as updates to the software happen, the examples just don't apply anymore. To avoid that, the examples used in this chapter will be hosted as Gists, in addition to being available to download form `apress.com`. This concept will be used where possible and deemed appropriate throughout the book, so look out for the references, but they'll be explained as they're used.

If the concept of a Gist is new to you, then it's just a code snippet that's hosted on GitHub, so they'll always be available. It also means the snippets can be altered and updated, so the code in the Gist should always work. If you discover it doesn't anymore, just leave a comment and then I can update the code so it functions again. This also means a full revision history will be kept, so if the code is for a different version it can be referenced in the change to show the version differences and so on. The sample in this book should be useful well after it's printed, which is always a bonus. Until the book is published all Gists will be kept private, but after the publish date they'll be made public.

Common pitfalls

When a technology exists for long enough, people get very good at using it, which brings wisdom and builds a list of Dos and Don'ts for the future. Neo4j is no different, and there are certain things that should be avoided, mainly performance issues. It can also be that the wrong data structure is being used and it needs to be streamlined. Either way, here are some common pitfalls and how to avoid them.

bi-directional relationships

There are many cases when a relationship goes both ways, and in most cases you don't care which way it goes, just as long as it exists. Since this can't be modelled in Neo4j, it can be avoided by only using one relationship. In the case of two brothers, you could model this relationship in a number of ways. One obvious example would be something like this:

```
(chris)-[:RELATED_TO]->(kane)
(kane)-[:RELATED_TO]->(chris)
```

Since both are related to each other, it makes sense for the relationship to go both ways, right? Yes, and there are cases when it's required. You may well use the relationship to store certain properties (In this example, it could have been {relation: "bother"}) but in a lot of cases the same data is stored twice, as it's assumed that having the context in both directions makes sense. The following structure results in the same problem:

```
(chris)-[:KICKED_BUTT {name: "Mario Kart", date: timestamp()}]->(kane)
(kane)-[:GOT_BUTT_KICKED {name: "Mario Kart", date: timestamp()}]->(chris)
```

This is done to ensure all of the context is kept, but the data in both is again the same. The only thing that changes is the relationship name. To avoid these problems, you simply need to have the node in one direction, and that's it. Thanks to Cypher, the direction of a relationship doesn't need to matter, as you don't need to specify one because the directions can go both ways. This means that instead of having two relationships, you have one, and then just don't specify a direction in the query. The first example changed to work this way would look like so:

```
(chris)-[:RELATED_TO {relation: "Brother"}]->(kane)
```

In this case the direction is pointing from `chris` to `kane` but that doesn't matter (It's because I'm older that it's not the other way around, but again, it doesn't matter) because as long as the relationship exists, that's enough. The property mentioned also got added in this case, so all the context required can be from a Cypher query, which would be:

```
MATCH (a:Person)-[r:RELATED_TO]-(b)
WHERE r.relation = "Brother"
RETURN a.name, b.name
```

The example would return two rows, each with "Chris" and "Kane" alternating as `a` and `b` for each row. The second example doesn't really change, as the second relationship simply isn't needed. You can imply that somebody got their butt kicked, or kicked butt depending on how the data is returned, so the other direction isn't needed.

The only real issue with this approach is that the data structure wouldn't be even, in the sense that the relationship would only be from one node, and not both. So, if you like symmetry, you'll need to resist the urge here (I'm one of those people, so I do it too) and just remember that Cypher has enough power to make the direction of the relationship not always required, and that in some cases (or all cases in real-life applications) one relationship is enough.

Using this method also requires less data, so it keeps your database smaller, and keeps queries cleaner.

Example Data Structures

With these example data structures, there will also be hints on how these can be used in real applications, so hopefully they can be tailored to your needs, and also benefit an application they're used in, while still being a reference on how to structure data.

e-commerce

One very big area that takes huge advantage of recommendations through relationships is e-commerce, so we'll run through a basic structure for that kind of application. Although the chunks of this example will be broken up, all of the queries can be found in a Gist (ADD_GIST_URL_HERE), so any updates will be available there. With that out of the way, let's begin. It's worth noting that this is a very basic structure, with just enough information to give an idea of how to structure the data and then expand on it for your own needs. Table 5-1 contains the different node types that will be used with this example.

Table 5-1. *e-commerce example node types and description*

Node type (Label)	Explanation
Customer	These are the customers of the application, so any information needed would be stored, name, e-mail, that kind of thing.
Product	Products will have any properties needed, but at the very least a name.
Category	Categories can be used to group products together of similar type.
Order	An order will attach to the products it contains and the customer that created it.
Bundle	Products that can be sold together as one unit.
Sale	A Sale will contain many Products, essentially like a Bundle. In this case though, it's a collection of products that all have their own prices, rather than 1 set price.

To get off to a good start, we know at least two things that need to be unique, the e-mail address of the user, and the uuid of the product. As has been mentioned before, this example only has the bare-bones of information, but even so, we can still add constraints, first the e-mail of the `Customer` node:

```
CREATE CONSTRAINT ON (c:Customer) ASSERT c.email IS UNIQUE;
```

Followed by the uuid constraint on the `Product` nodes

```
CREATE CONSTRAINT ON (p:Product) ASSERT p.uuid IS UNIQUE;
```

Although this example won't have any conflicting nodes, at least if the structure is extended in actual use, the constraints are already in place. Next up, let's add in some nodes:

```
CREATE (product1:Product {name: "Product 1", uuid: "d8d177cc-1542-11e5-b60b-1697f925ec7b", price: 10})
CREATE (product2:Product {name: "Product 2", uuid: "d8d17b28-1542-11e5-b60b-1697f925ec7b", price: 20})
CREATE (product3:Product {name: "Product 3", uuid: "d8d17c72-1542-11e5-b60b-1697f925ec7b", price: 30})
CREATE (product4:Product {name: "Product 4", uuid: "d8d1b958-1542-11e5-b60b-1697f925ec7b", price: 40})
CREATE (product5:Product {name: "Product 5", uuid: "d8d1bade-1542-11e5-b60b-1697f925ec7b", price: 50})
```

Here we just have some products being added, with various names, prices, and unique UUIDs, nothing too crazy here. Next up are the categories:

```
CREATE (category1:Category {name: "Category 1"})
CREATE (category2:Category {name: "Category 2"})
CREATE (category3:Category {name: "Category 3"})
```

Here the categories are just given a name, and referenced for later use in the query. There's a bundle in this example, so let's create that:

```
CREATE (bundle1:Bundle {name: "Bundle 1", price: 35})
```

The bundle here is created with a name, and also a price so we know how much the bundle sells for. Nothing can be sold until there are some customers, so let's add a couple:

```
CREATE (customer1:Customer {name: "Chris", email: "hey@chrisdkemper.co.uk"})
CREATE (customer2:Customer {name: "Kane", email: "thebrother@chrisdkemper.co.uk"})
```

The customers are created, with a unique e-mail address to ensure they adhere to the constraint placed earlier. Of course this data would all be dynamically created and related normally, but for the sake of example it's manually added. It's time to relate the newly created nodes now, starting with the products:

```
CREATE UNIQUE (product1)-[:BELONGS_TO]->(category1)
CREATE UNIQUE (product2)-[:BELONGS_TO]->(category1)
CREATE UNIQUE (product3)-[:BELONGS_TO]->(category2)
CREATE UNIQUE (product4)-[:BELONGS_TO]->(category3)
CREATE UNIQUE (product5)-[:BELONGS_TO]->(category2)
```

The incrementing product aliases would still be valid to use if all of the snippets were run together, which is why they'll be used in the different parts of the example. Each of the products is assigned to a category with the `BELONGS_TO` relationship. A product could be part of multiple categories as well, it just isn't in this instance. We also have a couple of products in a bundle, so those relationships need to added, and are like so:

```
CREATE UNIQUE (product1)-[:PART_OF]->(bundle1)
CREATE UNIQUE (product3)-[:PART_OF]->(bundle1).
```

`product1` and `product3` are part of this bundle, which is expressed with the `PART_OF` relationship. The final relationship to add is a sub category, which will be added like so:

```
CREATE UNIQUE (category3)-[:CHILD_OF]->(category1)
```

Here `category3` is actually a child of `category1`, which is shown by using the `CHILD_OF` relationship going in the correct direction. With the relationships now added, it's now possible to query the database to have a look at the structure in the Neo4j Browser using `MATCH (n) RETURN n`, the result of which can be seen in Figure 5-1.

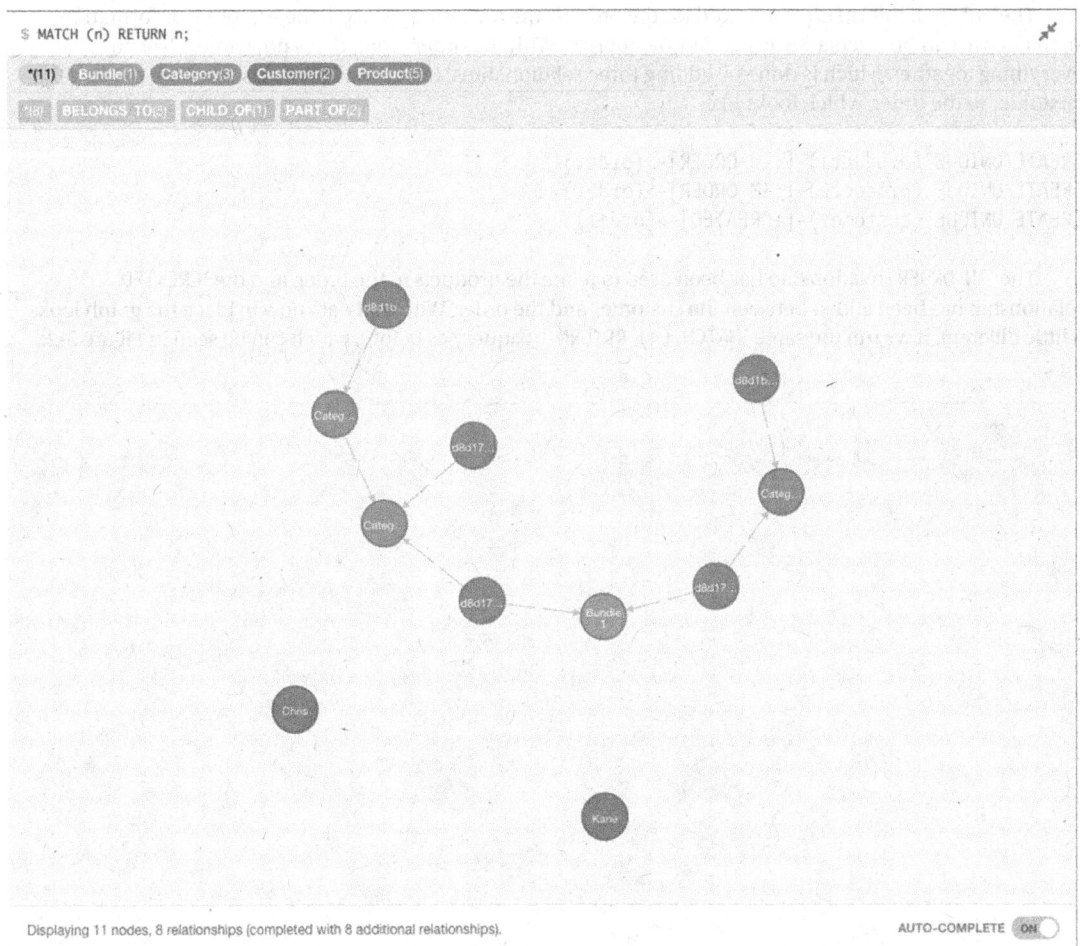

Figure 5-1. *An example data structure taking into account categories, products, bundles, and some customers (with no orders)*

It's already possible to see how the data will develop, but for now there aren't any orders yet, so we better add one. Since adding an order will be a new query to adding the data, to use the nodes required, they need to be matched, so let's do that first:

```
MATCH (customer:Customer {email: "hey@chrisdkemper.co.uk"})
      ,(product1:Product {uuid: "d8d177cc-1542-11e5-b60b-1697f925ec7b"})
      ,(product2:Product {uuid: "d8d17b28-1542-11e5-b60b-1697f925ec7b"})
```

This chunk of Cypher will match the products included in the order, and also the customer that made the order, so here we have `product1`, `product2` and the customer, respectively. Now that the nodes have been found, the order itself can be created, which is added like so:

```
CREATE (order:Order {date: "2015-05-15"})
```

The only real information required for the order is the date it was placed, the rest of the information, such as cost, can be calculated as needed via queries. With the order created, it's now time to relate everything together, which is done by adding three relationships, two for the products, and one relating the customer to the order, which looks like:

```
CREATE UNIQUE (product1)-[:IN_ORDER]->(order)
CREATE UNIQUE (product2)-[:IN_ORDER]->(order)
CREATE UNIQUE (customer)-[:CREATED]->(order)
```

The `IN_ORDER` relationship has been used to relate the products to the order, and the `CREATED` relationship has been added between the customer and the order. With that data now in place the graph looks a little different, if we run the same `MATCH (n) RETURN n;` query as before, which can be seen in Figure 5-2.

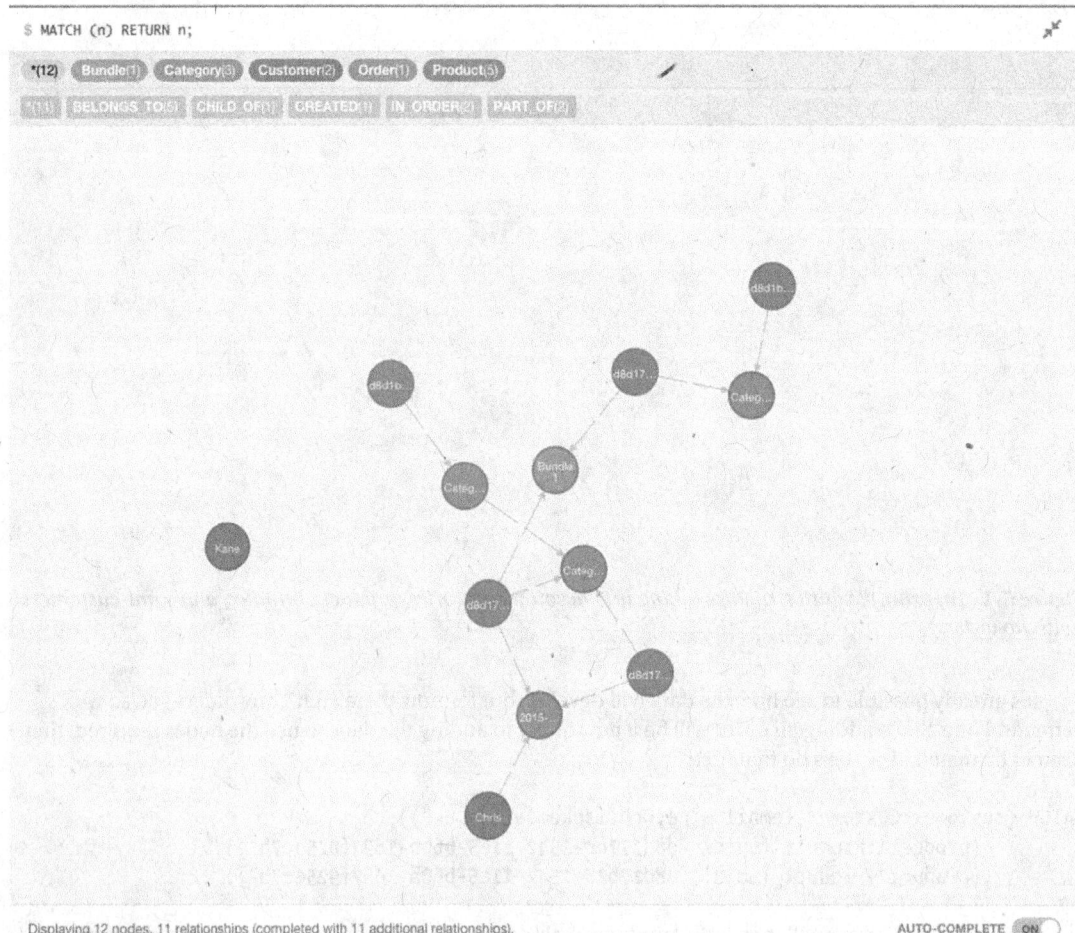

Figure 5-2. With new data added the graph looks a little different

Even with one order, we can already see that `Chris` has a preferred category, which means this information can be used in Cypher queries to generate recommendations on products that may be useful, potentially because they're on sale. Speaking of Sales, let's add one:

```
CREATE UNIQUE (sale1:Sale {name: "Sale 1", active: TRUE})
```

The sale here only really needs a name or some kind of identifier, as the information that matters can be added to the relationship between the `Product` and the `Sale`, which in this case, is the price.

```
MATCH (product4:Product {uuid: "d8d1b958-1542-11e5-b60b-1697f925ec7b"}),(product5:Product
{uuid: "d8d1bade-1542-11e5-b60b-1697f925ec7b"})
CREATE UNIQUE (product4)-[:ON_SALE {price: 36}]->(sale1)
CREATE UNIQUE (product5)-[:ON_SALE {price: 45}]->(sale1)
```

The products are first matched so the relationships can be added, then they are. In this case, a property of `price` is being added, with the price the item is on sale for. This could then be recovered when querying the data, and replace the price returned from the actual product, if the product happens to be on sale.

When more and more orders are added to the database, it becomes easy to detect trends. These trends can be that a customer buys more items from a certain category at certain times, or always buys a particular product. With this kind of data in hand, it's possible to craft very unique and tailored experiences for the user, based on their own data, so you get recommendations that actual work.

This code will be available in a whole via the GitHub Gist at https://gist.github.com/chrisdkemper/794416dbae1bb17942b1 so check there for any updates or changes to the example since the book has been published. Alternatively, all my Gists can be found at https://gist.github.com/chrisdkemper, so if you don't fancy typing the URL out, visit there first.

Social Network

Another big area that takes advantage of the power of graph databases is the social network side of things. Thanks to social networks, especially the giant that is Facebook, you can get in touch with somebody on the opposite side of the world through a friend, or a friend of a friend. When it comes to social graphs, it's all about who you know or who knows you; it's all about the common connections. Depending on what kind of social network you're building, the common connections could be interests, what somebody does for a living, hobbies, or anything.

In this case, we'll be using a basic example that will include: people, animals, and companies. As with the other example, the code for this one will be available as a GitHub gist, so any updates to the code will be available there, should anything change.

For this example, we'll be making a mini social network structure, involving people, companies, and animals. This will give a lot of potential for connections and relationships, and at least it's a little different from the usual social network stuff, eh? To start things off, Table 5-2 outlines the different labels that'll be used for nodes.

Table 5-2. *Social network node types and description*

Node type (Label)	Explanation
Company	A company is as it suggests, a company will be owned by a person or persons, and people can also work there.
Person	The main part of the social graph, people.
Animal	This label will be applied to any animal node, but in addition a label for the type, such as 'Dog' will also be added to give some extra context.

Although there aren't as many types in this example, there are a lot of relationships that can exist, and you don't always need a lot of node types to create a complex dataset. When the code is present on the Gist, it'll be commented as required, with different sections outlined, and instructions to run certain parts in isolation.

It's always good practice to create constraints, so let's do this here with the `Person` names to ensure they're always unique:

```
CREATE CONSTRAINT ON (p:Person) ASSERT p.name IS UNIQUE;
```

Also, in our case we aren't allowed to use companies with the same name either, so let's add that constraint in too:

```
CREATE CONSTRAINT ON (c:Company) ASSERT c.name IS UNIQUE;
```

With the constraints in place it's time to get some data into the database, starting with a number of `Persons`, six of them to be exact:

```
CREATE (person1:Person {name: "Chris"})
CREATE (person2:Person {name: "Kane"})
CREATE (person3:Person {name: "Dave"})
CREATE (person4:Person {name: "Claire"})
CREATE (person5:Person {name: "Ruth"})
CREATE (person6:Person {name: "Charlotte"})
```

This gives us a good number of people to work with. In this case it's just been kept simple with names, but you could easily add additional properties, if desired. With the people in place, let's add some animals to make things a bit more interesting.

```
CREATE (animal1:Animal:Dog {name: "Rolo"})
CREATE (animal2:Animal:Fish {name: "Totoro"})
CREATE (animal3:Animal:Fish {name: "Elsa"})
CREATE (animal4:Animal:Dog {name: "Ki"})
CREATE (animal5:Animal:Dog {name: "Rio"})
```

Here we have a number of animals, five in total, three dogs, and two fish. Each one is still an animal though, so if you ever wanted to find out the total number of animals, it saves having to add all the individual label counts together to get the total. You'll notice the additional labels are chained with `:`s, which creates the node with both labels. Finally, we need some companies to work with, so let's add those in:

```
CREATE (company1:Company {name: "Badass company"})
CREATE (company2:Company {name: "Supercorp"})
CREATE (company3:Company {name: "All of the things"})
```

Finally we have our companies, but without any relationships, these are just nodes in the database, so we'll start with relating people to their animals, with an `OWNS` relationship.

```
CREATE UNIQUE (person1)-[:OWNS]->(animal4)
CREATE UNIQUE (person1)-[:OWNS]->(animal5)
CREATE UNIQUE (person2)-[:OWNS]->(animal4)
CREATE UNIQUE (person2)-[:OWNS]->(animal5)
CREATE UNIQUE (person4)-[:OWNS]->(animal2)
CREATE UNIQUE (person4)-[:OWNS]->(animal3)
CREATE UNIQUE (person6)-[:OWNS]->(animal1)
```

You'll notice there are some multiples here. In this case, there's shared ownership of some of the animals, so the relationships are doubled up, but since they only go one way, it doesn't hit the bi-directional issue mentioned earlier. Having pets is great, but sometimes your pet can be more known than you. I know If I'm ever walking my dog and my brother's friends see him, they'll come up to me and say hello, even though I have no idea who they are, but since they know my dog, they apparently know me. Now let's add in some relationships to link together certain people by various means.

```
CREATE UNIQUE (person1)-[:RELATED_TO]->(person2)
CREATE UNIQUE (person1)-[:FRIENDS_WITH]->(person6)
CREATE UNIQUE (person2)-[:KNOWS]->(person3)
CREATE UNIQUE (person4)-[:FRIENDS_WITH]->(person2)
CREATE UNIQUE (person5)-[:KNOWS]->(animal4)
```

Here we have a mix of relationships, from `RELATED_TO` to `FRIENDS_WITH` between both `Person` and `Animal` nodes. I'm sure there are many people that you may know, or know of, but aren't friends with, and that's what is being illustrated here. There's nothing to say that later down the line, a `KNOWS` relationship goes to a `FRIENDS_WITH` or even a `DATING` relationship, who knows?!

With our people and animals related, it's time to sort out the companies. In this case, we have owners, and employees, and for one company, a mascot. First things first, let's set up the owners:

```
CREATE UNIQUE (person1)-[:FOUNDED]->(company3)
CREATE UNIQUE (person3)-[:FOUNDED]->(company2)
CREATE UNIQUE (person6)-[:FOUNDED]->(company1)
```

The `FOUNDED` relationship has been used here, but there could easily be additional properties for dates, or any other related information, if it was needed. Now the companies have been founded, employees are needed, so let's add those now:

```
CREATE UNIQUE (person2)-[:WORKS_AT]->(company3)
CREATE UNIQUE (person4)-[:WORKS_AT]->(company2)
CREATE UNIQUE (person5)-[:WORKS_AT]->(company1)
```

Using the `WORKS_AT` relationship here to show which people work at which company. Again, there's always the option for additional context, such as hours or pay, if it were needed. Finally, because I can, my dog is the mascot of my company, so let's add that relationship:

```
CREATE UNIQUE (animal4)-[:MASCOT_OF]->(company1)
```

With all that data in place, it creates a graph that makes extensive use of Relationships (Figure 5-3).

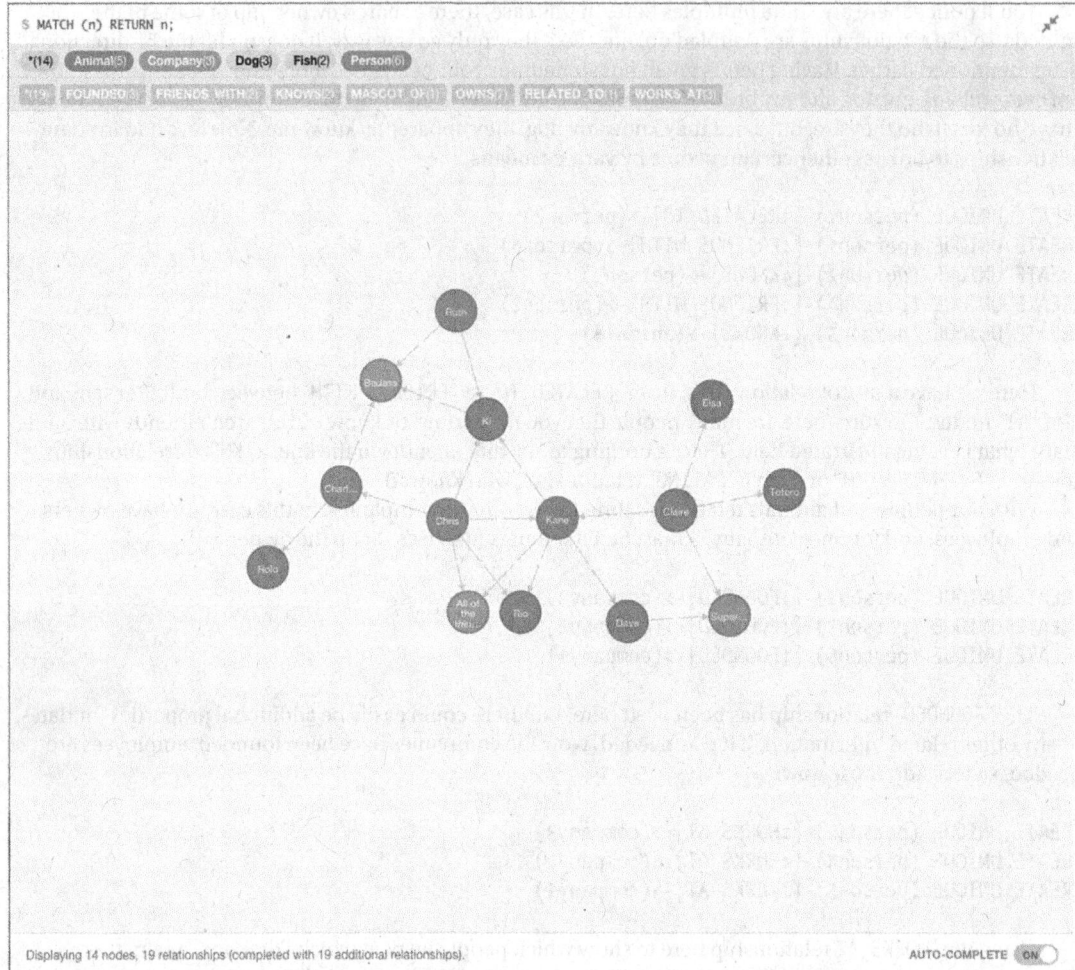

Figure 5-3. *A preview of the data structure created for the theoretical social network, which has animals, people, and companies*

Even with this small amount of data, it's possible to see how close some of the `Person` nodes are, so with some simple queries, it could easily recommend new friends, or even a new place to work. Using information like this you could see which company your friends and family work for, and whose pet is the most popular.

With more data, this would increase the potential connections in the database, and with new animals and companies, it would start to create a social graph that'd make finding new friends and/or opportunities easy.

As mentioned earlier, the code used to create this demo will be available via GitHub on the Gist (https://gist.github.com/chrisdkemper/8c981b759275ec36d3bf) so any changes or updates will be made available there, or just check out https://gist.github.com/chrisdkemper for all of my Gists.

Summary

In this chapter we've been through some common pitfalls when structuring data in Neo4j, as well as some example structures. Hopefully these can be used to give an idea on how you can structure your own application to allow for better connections, less clutter, and therefore a better database experience. There is a lack of complex Cypher queries in this chapter, but don't worry, in the Chapter 7, we'll be taking some of the lessons learned here a step further, to show how it's possible to create things like recommendations based on an existing dataset.

CHAPTER 6

Importing and Exporting Data

Unless you're starting an application from scratch, odds are you're going to need to import data into Neo4j to work with. There are a number of ways to do this, so we'll go through a number of these, and also, how to get your data out of Neo4j, if you want to do that, anyway.

Since you can't export data if you don't have any in the first place, let's start with importing data, shall we?

Importing Data

As mentioned before, there are a number of ways to import data into Neo4j, the easiest of which is to just write the needed Cypher code to import the nodes you need. In the last chapter, this technique was used to create some basic data structures, and it can be used in any other application to do the same. This approach does has a number of advantages, including instant feedback. If you made an error in your code, you accidentally type something wrong, or there is some other issue, this can be seen straight away, especially if you return the created node after the query.

Using the browser to import data also allows you to see how the data is shaping up, as you can import the data in chunks and relate it as needed. This is the process used in the previous chapter, and provided you aren't importing 100s or 1000s of nodes (that'd be a lot of queries) then this method will work just fine.

Import from a CSV Using Cypher

If you have your data in a nice CSV format (Or you can convert your data to CSV) then Neo4j can help you out. There is a built-in Cypher command that allows data to be imported from a CSV, with a number of options to tailor the import for your needs. A CSV can be loaded via https, http, ftp, and file:// so whether your file is remote or local, it can be used.

Before diving right in and importing the CSV, it's a good idea to ensure the CSV is valid. If there's a problem with your CSV, then it may cause issues with the import, so it's best to rule out issues with the CSV by validating it. This is especially important when you aren't the one who generated the CSV. There are a number of tools available to validate CSVs, so this process can be easy, if there aren't any errors to fix, that is.

CSV Lint

This tool, which can be found online at csvlint.io, allows you to validate your CSV to check for errors, from either a remote or local file. Not only does the site check for validation errors in the CSV, it also gives you recommendations on how to make it better. For example, if you're hosting your CSV and it's being served with the wrong content header, it'll mention this, and give a recommendation on how to solve it. An example of this can be seen in Figure 6-1, which is based on the CSV used in the Neo4j documentation.

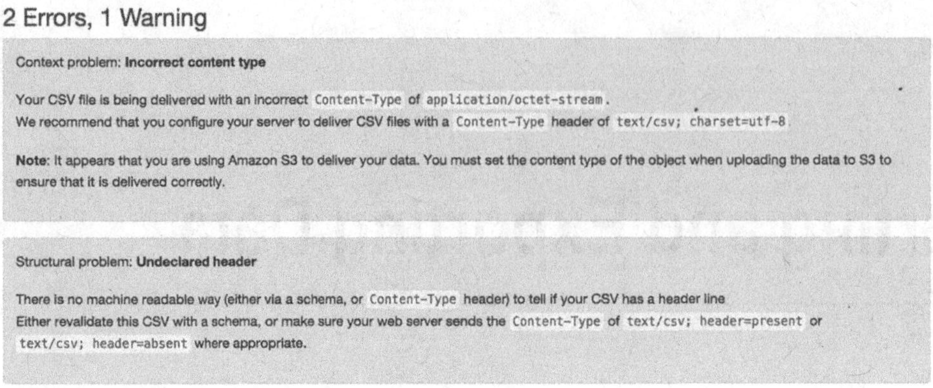

2 Errors, 1 Warning

Context problem: **Incorrect content type**

Your CSV file is being delivered with an incorrect `Content-Type` of `application/octet-stream`.
We recommend that you configure your server to deliver CSV files with a `Content-Type` header of `text/csv; charset=utf-8`.

Note: It appears that you are using Amazon S3 to deliver your data. You must set the content type of the object when uploading the data to S3 to ensure that it is delivered correctly.

Structural problem: **Undeclared header**

There is no machine readable way (either via a schema, or `Content-Type` header) to tell if your CSV has a header line
Either revalidate this CSV with a schema, or make sure your web server sends the `Content-Type` of `text/csv; header=present` or
`text/csv; header=absent` where appropriate.

Figure 6-1. *Recommendations after using csvlint.io to validate a CSV*

The two errors mentioned in Figure 6-1 are both related to how the file is being served from the server. The first is essentially saying, the file is being served with a vague content header. The one being used here is "application/octet-stream" which is a binary file, but since there's a header for CSV "text/csv" then this should be used, as it's way more specific. The second error is referencing the header row of the CSV (so all of the column headings) and whether or not it's present. Tools that use CSVs will generally have to work out if there is a header row present within the file or not, but if the correct header is sent, then this check won't need to be done. If you know your CSV has a row of column headings, then make sure to use "text/csv; header=present" when serving the file, and "text/csv; header=absent" if not.

As well as this feedback to help clean up your CSV, there's also an option to "Download standardized CSV" which gives an option to download a CSV that has the errors fixed. Of course, it'd be recommended to again, check the CSV it gives you to ensure the structure of the data is correct, and it's still in the same format that was initially desired. Of course, you can keep using the site to check for errors until your CSV is clean and ready to use.

This tool is currently in alpha (at the time of writing it is, anyway) but it is still very helpful to get some useful feedback on your CSV file, especially with the service being hosted. If you're authoring your own CSV rather than exporting it, then there's also some good advice on writing CSVs that can be found at `http://csvlint.io/about` to help make the process even easier.

Papa Parse

This CSV tool is downloaded rather than hosted, but has a lot of features that make that worth it. You can find Papa Parse on GitHub at `https://github.com/mholt/PapaParse` and also at `papaparse.com`. This tool is written as JavaScript and can be run in the browser. It has quite comprehensive documentation, and also an interactive demo page (`http://papaparse.com/demo`) which can be used to test out the features it has. Speaking of features, it has a good list of them a section of which can be seen in Table 6-1.

Table 6-1. *Some of the features of Papa Parse*

Feature	Explanation
CSV→JSON and JSON→CSV	You have the ability to convert a CSV to JSON, but also to convert from JSON to CSV, so there's a lot of freedom there.
File handling	Papa Parse can handle files in a number of ways. You can open a local file, or even download a remote one. If your file is rather large, it may be worthwhile to stream it rather than just straight downloading it, and Papa Parse can handle that too.
Auto-detect delimiter	This is very useful when working with CSVs, as the delimiter can differ from the standard comma and be anything, but Papa Parse can work that out for you.
Multi-threaded	If a file is parsing for a long time, it could make the page non-responsive. To get around this, it's possible to use a worker, which will keep the page active.
Header row support	Whether or not your CSV has a header row, Papa parse can work with that. If you tell it you have a header row, the data will be keyed by it; otherwise indexes will be used.
Type conversion	Unless you state otherwise, everything in the CSV will be parsed as a string, as this is the safest way to deal with data, because everything can be a string. If this isn't good enough, `dynamicTyping` can be turned on within Papa Parse, and any booleans or integers that are detected will be parsed as the correct type, and not string.
Graceful error handling	If your CSV happens to have errors in the rows, then it'll try it's best to carry on, then returns stats of the failed row when the import is complete. Rather than just a vague error, Papa Parse will give a reason it couldn't parse a row, and also the number, so any errors can be manually addressed if needed.

The demo on the website can actually be used to parse data passed to it, but this will only work for small amounts of data, but for optimal results, it'd be better to run Papa Parse locally which gives more flexibility on the features used. Using Papa Parse allows you to validate your CSV before using it with Cypher, but it also means you can use it to convert JSON data to a CSV, which means that the data can then be imported with Cypher, and used within Neo4j, which is a bonus.

Load a CSV into Cypher

With a valid CSV now in place, it's time to actually use it with Cypher. To import the CSV, the LOAD CSV clause will be used in Cypher, which can load a file from either a local filesystem, or a remote endpoint. If you're hosting your file, it could be worth testing it before trying to import it, if you haven't already, that is. When working with local files, there are a couple of rules that need to be respected. First, if your file is local, you must declare the file:// protocol directly, and then build the path up from '/' on the machine. On OSX/ UNIX, you would need to use the following for a local file "file:///path/to/data.csv" whereas the same url on Windows would be "file:c:/path/to/data.csv". It can be a bit tricky to get these right sometimes, especially if you're using a virtual environment. The way around this (and the easier option for loading CSVs) is to load the file over HTTP, which can be a remote, or local file.

To load a CSV locally, some form of web server will be required to run on `localhost` to serve the file. When the server is running on localhost, just place the file in the root of the directory being used by the server, which will allow it to be loaded via "`http://localhost/data.csv`". Of course, if the file cannot be in the root, simply adjust the URL as needed, or it's easier to host the file remotely, just replace the local address with a remote one, and Cypher will work in the same way.

If you're unsure whether or not Cypher will be able to run the file, then don't worry, you can test the CSV without having to import anything. By using a simple Cypher query, you can read the first few rows from the CSV, which will either show the rows on success, or give an error on failure. The query in question is as follows:

```
LOAD CSV FROM "http://localhost/file.csv" AS row WITH row
RETURN row
LIMIT 5;
```

You can also just get a count of the rows in the CSV to double-check things, which can be done like so:

```
LOAD CSV FROM "http://localhost/file.csv" AS line WITH row
RETURN COUNT(*);
```

If Cypher cannot load the file, you will receive a message telling you the resource cannot be loaded, with an error code of `Neo.TransientError.Statement.ExternalResourceFailure`, so if you get an error, you'll know straight away. Being able to review the first few lines of the CSV is useful for a number of reasons, the same goes for the row count, too. It allows you to ensure the file is in the expected location first, but then allows you to see what Cypher classes in are the first few rows, or the total number of rows, depending on your need. If you see in the preview that there seems to be an error in the rows, or something doesn't seem right, it means the CSV can be reviewed, and potentially fixed before it's imported, which leads to less errors overall.

One thing that can cause an issue is the use of a non-standard delimiter, which would mean the rows won't be interpreted properly by Cypher, as by default it looks for a comma separator. For argument's sake, let's assume this CSV has a non-standard separator, so rather than a comma, a semi-colon is being used.

If a LOAD CSV query was run without telling Neo4j what the delimiter was, then it'd assume it was a comma, and therefore would fail, or get some very odd results if it didn't. In some cases, it's easier to use a different delimiter than to escape all of the commas in your file, so if you were importing big chunks of text, a different delimiter other than a comma would be helpful. Anyway, to tell Cypher you're using a non-standard delimiter, just add the FIELDTERMINATOR cause to the query, which looks like so:

```
LOAD CSV FROM "http://localhost/file.csv" AS line WITH line  FIELDTERMINATOR ';'
```

Now, when the CSV is processed it'll pick up the correct delimiter and process the file correctly, which is what we want. With the correct delimiter now specified, the data can be tested to ensure it works correctly, so the previous query can be reused to test the file again before it's imported, which is done like so:

```
LOAD CSV FROM "http://localhost/file.csv" AS line WITH line FIELDTERMINATOR ';'
RETURN line
LIMIT 5;
```

Process the CSV

At this stage, the CSV being used should be valid, and in the correct location, so it's finally ready to start importing the contents into Neo4j. With this example, I'll be using a locally hosted CSV as that's the easiest way to load it, or at least for me, anyway. The CSV in question is a list of people with a number of properties. Rather than listing them all, the contents of the CSV is as follows:

```
id,First Name,Middle name(s),Surname,D.O.B,Favourite Animal ,Favourite Colour,friend_id
1,Chris,D.,Kemper,28/11/88,Dog,Red,2
2,Kane,Phil,Scott,2/10/90,Dog,Yellow,
3,Dave,,James,5/5/75,Shark,Pink,1
5,Claire,North,West,20/2/70,Fish,Green,
8,Andy,,Green,19/1/80,Dog,Purple,3
9,Charlotte,Sue,Lee,7/5/88,Giraffe,Orange,12
10,Sterling,Mallory,Archer,5/9/48,Ocelot,Blue,
11,Peter,,Gray,10/7/90,Snake,Red,10
12,Sarah,Jennifer,Mitchell,15/9/80,Cat,Yellow,
```

The data being specified here is a list of people with various attributes attached, such as a date of birth, and a favorite animal. For ease, I'll be hosting the CSV locally, so it can be accessed over localhost. In this case, this CSV will only require the creation of one label, Person, which means when it comes to importing the nodes, the query is nice and simple.

Before importing data, it's always a good idea to create some constraints on the data, to ensure certain properties are always unique. Adding contrasts also gives another benefit that we know of already, in the form of creating an index, which helps make getting the data out of Neo4j a lot faster. Let's create a constraint on this data for good measure. Since we're dealing with people, there are chances for duplication on pretty much every field, as people do have the same name, and also like the same things, so constraints shouldn't be added on those, unless your application requires otherwise, of course. There is an Id column in the file here, which is required to be unique, so a constraint works perfectly here:

```
CREATE CONSTRAINT ON (p:Person) ASSERT p.id IS UNIQUE;
```

With the constraint place, the data is now ready to be imported and you can be confident the id of each person will be unique, which is just what we want for the import.

That data now needs to be imported by using LOAD CSV, but in this case, with the addition of WITH HEADERS. This allows for the CSVs headers to be referenced by their keys in the query, which makes things easier than using index. If you were to load a CSV without headers, instead of using the column header you would just use the index, so the first would be 0, and then moving up from there. To reference the index, just treat the variable like an array, so you'd index a row by using square brackets. If you've aliased the CSV row with 'AS row`, to use a value from that row via an index, it would be row[0], rather than row.name, for example. A full example would look something like the following, depending on your data.

```
LOAD CSV WITH HEADERS FROM 'http://localhost/people.csv' AS row
CREATE (:Person {
        id: row.id,
        first_name: row.`First Name`,
        middle_name: row.`Middle name(s)`,
        surname: row.`Surname`,
        dob: row.`D.O.B`,
        favourite_animal: row.`Favourite Animal`,
        favourite_colour: row.`Favourite Colour`
})
```

It's also possible to assign properties using the SET clause, rather than having one big CREATE. The same result as above can be converted to use SET like so:

```
CREATE (p:Person {id: row.id})
SET p.first_name: row.`First Name`
        p.middle_name: row.`Middle name(s)`,
        p.surname: row.`Surname`,
        p.dob: row.`D.O.B`,
        p.favourite_animal: row.`Favourite Animal`,
        p.favourite_colour: row.`Favourite Colour`
})
```

The main difference here (other than the use of SET, of course) is that before the alias for the node was emitted as it wasn't needed (so just :Person) whereas here, it's `p`. This is so that the same node can be used later in the query to have values assigned to it, using (you guessed it) SET. Using SET can make your code easier to lay out, and if you need to use any functions on the data (such as TOINT()), this keeps each property on its own line, making the code easy to read, which is always a bonus.

Running either of these queries will give the same results, and will import all of the nodes using the values from the CSV, creating a node and then applying properties to it, and even though the data in the CSV is unique and will import fine, if two nodes had the same id, the second would fail as that id is taken. This data sample is quite small, but what if you want to import a large amount of rows? Well, if you want to import large amounts of data, you'll need to make at least one change, potentially two, depending on how Neo4j is set up. The first thing is to ensure Neo4j has enough RAM to be able to process the import.

■ **Note**   When it comes to importing, the more RAM the better, as it'll make your import faster. You'll want to have 3–4GB of RAM allocated to Neo4j, but if you can assign more then do that. To update the amount Neo4j has at its disposal, the `neo4j-wrapper.conf` must be modified, which is located within the `conf` directory of Neo4j. The properties we're looking to update are `wrapper.java.initmemory` and `wrapper.java.maxmemory`.

What's actually being updated here is the amount allocated to Java heap, but there's also another set of memory values that need to be updated, which are the memory-mapping values. When you're doing an import, data is stored within these two locations so it can be reused within the remaining parts of the import. This is why more RAM is better, as it means more data can be stored within it, and the data doesn't need to be looked up again, which slows things down. Within the `neo4j.properties` file (within config, once again) the following values should be updated:

```
# Default values for the low-level graph engine
neostore.nodestore.db.mapped_memory=50M
neostore.relationshipstore.db.mapped_memory=500M
neostore.propertystore.db.mapped_memory=100M
neostore.propertystore.db.strings.mapped_memory=100M
neostore.propertystore.db.arrays.mapped_memory=0M
```

In these two places there is a total of 4.75GB of RAM required, but on a Windows machine, this is slightly different. On Unix-like systems and OS X, these two values are separate, whereas on Windows, they're one combined value. In this case, 750MB allocated to the memory-mapping will come out of the 4GB assigned for the Java heap, so if you're on Windows, be sure to update this value to be inclusive of both values. In this example, you'd set the value on Windows 750MB to 1GB higher to account for this.

With these values set and updated, Neo4j can now be restarted so these values can take effect. With the RAM sorted out it's time to make the other change, which is an optional one within Cypher. It's possible to run an import in batches rather than just in one go, which is achieved by using PERIODIC COMMIT. Using this clause wraps a transaction around however many rows are specified, which when you're dealing with a large amount of rows will be required for the import to be successful.

Using PERIODIC COMMIT is easy, and can be done with the addition of one line before LOAD CSV is called. If the previous example were to use PERIODIC COMMIT, it would look like so:

```
USING PERIODIC COMMIT 500
LOAD CSV WITH HEADERS FROM 'http://localhost/people.csv' AS row
CREATE (:Person {
        id: row.id,
        first_name: row.`First Name`,
        middle_name: row.`Middle name(s)`,
        surname: row.`Surname`,
        dob: row.`D.O.B`,
        favourite_animal: row.`Favourite Animal`,
        favourite_colour: row.`Favourite Colour`
})
```

With the addition on PERIODIC COMMIT it now means the query is done in 500 row batches. Now the CSV will be processed by transactions that will be committed every 500 rows. If you have more RAM at your disposal this value could be increased to 1000 (or even 10000) if required.

For each transaction, all of data will be stored in RAM, so if you don't have enough RAM to handle 1000 rows, then the import will fail. You can of course run lots of smaller transactions, but this will take a lot longer, so how many rows are handled within the transaction is totally dependent on the CSV size, and how the RAM for Neo4j is allocated.

Importing Relationships

When you're importing data, you may well also want to import relationships, and that can be achieved using LOAD CSV. To ensure the import is as efficient as possible, it's advised that creating nodes and relationships aren't done within the same query, so create your nodes first, and then relate them. Depending on how your data is set it, your relationships could either be in the same CSV as your nodes in the form of joining ids, or potentially in another file. In this case, our relationships are within the same file, so the first step is to use LOAD CSV once again, but this time to relate the nodes, rather than create them.

```
USING PERIODIC COMMIT 500
LOAD CSV WITH HEADERS FROM 'http://localhost/people.csv' AS row
MATCH (p:Person {id: row.id})
MATCH (friend:Person {id: row.friend_id})
MERGE (p)-[f:FRIENDS_WITH]->(friend)
WHERE row.friend_id IS NOT NULL;
```

Since this data has already been imported, reading the same CSV again means the data is all already there, so we can just use MATCH to bring back the related nodes. To avoid clogging up the database, the `friend_id` values were never imported, as they're only needed to relate the nodes. This way, the same CSV can just be used again, so any reference fields can be left in and not imported, which makes cleaner data.

The query itself is simple enough. We're matching the person and friend based on their Ids, but only where `friend_id` isn't null. This ensures the query is only applied when the values required for it to run are there, which reduces on errors, and for the sake of large files, saves time as it'll skip rows that aren't suitable.

Running an Update from a CSV

Although sometimes imports can be one-offs, this isn't always the case. It may well be that the client actually hadn't finished with the CSV when you imported it, and they've now added a bunch of new rows and updated some of the existing values. It may also be that because of how this system works, giving a client a CSV of data they can edit works out to be easier than getting it in another format. Regardless of the reason, there may come a time that you need to update existing Neo4j data via a CSV, and this is very possible.

To ensure we can create and update nodes, the previous query used will need to be modified. Otherwise Neo4j will attempt to create duplicate nodes, and then fail because of the constraint. The update Cypher code looks like the following:

```
LOAD CSV WITH HEADERS FROM 'http://localhost/people.csv' AS row
MERGE (p:Person { id: row.id })
ON CREATE SET
        p.first_name: row.`First Name`,
        p.middle_name: row.`Middle name(s)`,
        p.surname: row.`Surname`,
        p.dob: row.`D.O.B`,
        p.favourite_animal: row.`Favourite Animal`,
        p.favourite_colour: row.`Favourite Colour`
ON MATCH SET
        p.first_name: row.`First Name`,
        p.middle_name: row.`Middle name(s)`,
        p.surname: row.`Surname`,
        p.dob: row.`D.O.B`,
        p.favourite_animal: row.`Favourite Animal`,
        p.favourite_colour: row.`Favourite Colour`,
        p.updatedOn = timestamp()
```

The query looks very different, but that's for good reason. First, CREATE is no longer used, instead MERGE is. The MERGE clause is very powerful, and we can use it to create new nodes if needed, but then also update a node if it matches. In this query, it'll try to find a person by their id, if that person exists, it'll update the properties on that person with those from the CSV and also set an updated date. If the node doesn't exist, then it'll create a node with the specified properties. This is made possible thanks to the ON CREATE and ON MATCH clauses, which are one of the reasons MERGE is so powerful.

This query can now be used with a new CSV, or an existing one, as it does both updates and creates, which when you're working on an import, those are the actions you want to be able to accomplish.

Using a Custom Import Script

A CSV isn't always the best format to export your data and it's just easier to import the data using your choice of programming language. If the data being imported is actually an export from another system, it could be possible to have this in a more structured format, such as JSON. This means you can still iterate over the data, but it can be processed in whichever way suits the application.

The data being used may also be live, and Neo4j is simply being used to bring some additional functionality to an application, so frequent imports are required. If this is the case, then this live data may be available via an API or an HTTP endpoint. This means you could write an importer that checks the URL every day to see if there is any additional data. The data here would be structured in a way to make the import easier, so that you can create nodes, but also then create relationships too, as they're needed.

To allow for flexibility when importing data this way, it's important to create constraints on the database. This will ensure no duplicates happen, and keeps the queries fast as a constraint uses an INDEX under the hood, so it's a win/win. The constraints would also be needed to make relationships possible. To ensure the data can be as flexible as possible, you'd need to be confident that you wouldn't get duplicates, so that each relationship call worked as expected. A basic example of this would be as follows

```
[{
    "nodes" : [
        {
            "label" : ["Person"],
            "identifier" : "shortname",
            "properties" : [
                {
                    "name" : "name",
                    "value" : "Chris Kemper",
                    "type" : "string",
                },
                {
                    "name" : "shortname",
                    "value" : "chrisdkemper",
                    "type" : "string",
                }
            ]
        },
        {
            "label" : ["Person"],
            "identifier" : "shortname",
            "properties" : [
                {
                    "name" : "name",
                    "value" : "Kane Kemper",
                    "type" : "string",
                },
                {
                    "name" : "shortname",
                    "value" : "kjck",
                    "type" : "string",
                }
            ]
        }
    ],
    "relationships" : [
        {
            "type" : "RELATED",
            "nodes" : [
                {
                    "shortname" : "chrisdkemper"
                },
                {
                    "shortname" : "kjck"
                }
```

```
        ],
        "properties" : []
    }
  ]
}]
```

In the JSON here there are two arrays, nodes and relationships. In this case, the nodes within the nodes array would be created or updated, and once this process is finished, the relationships would be processed. Each node also has an identifier which can be used to look up the node to see if it exists, which in this case is the `shortname` property. The `shortname` would always be unique thanks to the constraint, so this can be relied on. If the node did exist, the properties contained within it would be updated, or if the node didn't exist it would be created with those properties.

The properties exist in an array format, as well as the type of the value, in this case they're both strings. This means if you had a particular field type, it could be parsed to ensure it's stored within Neo4j correctly. This isn't really an issue with strings as this is the default type, but for fields such as integers, the type would need to be explicitly set.

Within the relationship array, there is one item, which contains a type, nodes, and properties. The type here is in reference to the relationship type, and would be used in the same way as the `shortname` field to ensure the relationships are unique. The nodes portion of the JSON object contains information needed to search for the nodes and then relate them. In this case it's the `shortname` property and the corresponding values for the two nodes that will also be created. You'll notice no direction is specific here, and that's because the ordering of the nodes array dictates the direction, so in this case, the first node will be related to the second with an outward relationship. There is also a properties array here, which will be used to add properties to the relationship should they need to be added.

The code using this data would use Cypher queries to create the needed nodes and relationships, and also to query for existing items. How the code would interact with Cypher would be up to you, whether this is direct with Curl, or potentially using the neo4jphp Neo4j wrapper written in PHP, created by jadell (which can be found at `https://github.com/jadell/neo4jphp`) or something similar. With a connection to Neo4j in place the import would then iterate over the code, taking advantage of Cyphers MERGE and CREATE UNIQUE clauses to ensure the data is unique.

Having the data structured in this way allows for the importer using it to be used as often as you'd like, as the process will only create unique nodes, and the constraint will enforce this. Of course the logic for the importer can be completely custom and you may actually want to create duplicate nodes, in which case the constraints can be removed. This is the freedom that comes from creating your own importer, it also means you can reuse this as much as you'd like. It also means any desired changes can be made whenever they're required, which gives more flexibility than Cyphers' CSV import method, should you need it.

If you had a lot of projects that required data to be imported on a regular basis, it could also be useful to create a standalone application that could be included within your applications as and when it's needed. If a standalone application exists, it means it can be pulled down as needed and then removed to save space in the repository. If you happen to be building an open source application, or one that'll be shared online, bundling the importer with the code gives anybody using the project the option to import the data. Be sure to include documentation on how to use the importer if you do this though, so any unfamiliar users won't be caught out.

Exporting Data

At some point or another, there'll be a time when you want to export data from a Neo4j database. This could be for a backup, or even to use within another application, but at some point you'll no doubt want to export some, or all of the data within a database. There sadly isn't a way to just export the entirety of the database using the core Neo4j tools, but there are a couple of options.

Backing up the Database

If you're wanting to backup the data, or clone the database for use in another Neo4j application, then this is possible without too much hassle. The first step is to locate the database, which is set vía the `org.neo4j.server.database.location` property within the `neo4j-server.properties` file. Unless this value has been changed, it should be `data/graph.db` which on an Ubuntu machine, means the file is located at /var/lib/neo4j/data/graph.db. With the file located, the next step is to stop the Neo4j service from running so that the database won't change while you're copying it, which is done using the following command:

```
service neo4j-service stop
```

Depending on your setup, the use of `sudo` may be required at the start of the command, to get around any permission errors. If this is the case for you, some kind of permission error will be returned, such as:

```
start-stop-daemon: warning: failed to kill 1131: Operation not permitted
rm: cannot remove '/var/lib/neo4j/data/neo4j-service.pid': Permission denied
```

When the command runs successfully, nothing is returned. To double-check Neo4j definitely isn't running, you can use `service neo4j-service status` which will return the state of Neo4j, and what we're looking for is `* neo4j is not running`. Now that Neo4j isn't running, it's just a case of zipping up the directory, moving it to where it's needed, and then finally, starting Neo4j once again.

If you haven't done so already, cd into the directory containing the Neo4j db, which in my case is `/var/lib/neo4j/data/`. From within that directory, the graph.db directory needs to be zipped up somehow; one method is to use the following to turn the directory into a .tar file, and then, to zip that file, which is done using two commands.

```
tar -cvf graph.db.tar graph.db
```

This will create the `graph.db.tar` file for you, the next step is to zip this directory, which can be done using:

```
gzip graph.db.tar
```

This creates a `graph.db.tar.gz` file, and now all that's left is to move it to where it's needed, or store it as a backup. To get this file back to normal, the commands just need to be run in reverse. First, unzip the file using `gunzip graph.db.tar.gz` and then untar the file using `tar -xvf graph.db.tar`, which will leave you with a ready to use graph.db file.

There may again be a need to use `sudo` here if you don't have the needed permissions, so if you're presented with an error similar to the following, you'll need `sudo`.

```
tar: graph.db.tar: Cannot open: Permission denied
tar: Error is not recoverable: exiting now
```

Getting Data from the Neo4j Browser

When using the Browser that comes with Neo4j, you have the ability to export the results of Cypher queries to SVG, PNG, JSON, or CSV. This could be potentially used as an export method, however the query run would be custom depending on which data you wanted returned from the database. For example, say you wanted to export the entire database, a good start would be to run the following Cypher query, and then export the result, theoretically.

```
MATCH (n) RETURN n;
```

In the Browser this will return every node and relationship in the database, but if you were to export this query as JSON, you would be given the same response as if you had queried the database using Curl. An example of the output can be seen here:

```
{
  "columns": [
    "n"
  ],
  "data": [
    {
      "row": [
        {
          "name": "Chris"
        }
      ],
      "graph": {
        "nodes": [
          {
            "id": "171",
            "labels": [
              "Person"
            ],
            "properties": {
              "name": "Chris"
            }
          }
        ],
        "relationships": [

        ]
      }
    },
    {
      "row": [
        {
          "name": "Kane"
        }
      ],
      "graph": {
        "nodes": [
          {
            "id": "172",
            "labels": [
              "Person"
            ],
            "properties": {
              "name": "Kane"
            }
          }
        ],
        "relationships": [
```

```
          ]
        }
      }
    ],
    "stats": {
      "contains_updates": false,
      "nodes_created": 0,
      "nodes_deleted": 0,
      "properties_set": 0,
      "relationships_created": 0,
      "relationship_deleted": 0,
      "labels_added": 0,
      "labels_removed": 0,
      "indexes_added": 0,
      "indexes_removed": 0,
      "constraints_added": 0,
      "constraints_removed": 0
    }
  }
}
```

This data sample is from a database consisting of two nodes with `Person` labels, with the `name` property values of `Chris` and `Kane`, which are also related together with a `RELATED_TO` relationship. Each of the returned nodes is added as a result row, with the labels, and properties of that node included. There aren't however any relationships mentioned, so if you needed the data and the relationships, they would need to be explicitly returned. Although you may need everything included in the returned JSON, odds are you would only want the information on what is actually returned from the query, and in this case that's nodes.

If you were to return the data as a CSV rather than JSON, then the data returned would be different. An example of this can be seen below:

```
n
"{""name"":""Chris""}"
"{""name"":""Kane""}"
```

The first row of the CSV is the column heading, which matches the return value of `n` from the `MATCH (n) RETURN n;` query. The remaining rows of the file are JSON, but since this is a CSV file, the quotes have been escaped, so if you were to open this in a spreadsheet application, or parse it as a CSV, the JSON would then be valid. Using the CSV option does remove a lot of the clutter from the JSON response, but a lot of information is also lost, such as the labels for the nodes, and the actual id of the node.

Although both of these approaches can be used to export data via the Browser, each has their advantages, and disadvantages. The JSON export contains information that is potentially un-needed but is badly structured, and the CSV format loses some key information. Of course it is totally possible to then tailor the query using either export method, to ensure everything that you need to have returned, is returned.

This method of exporting data may not be perfect, but unless the browser has been explicitly disabled, it means that anytime a quick export is needed, it can be achieved with no additional tools through the Browser. In addition, if your particular export query ends up being quite complex, it can then be saved and used later to save on time and effort.

Write Your Own Data Exporter

Although other tools can make things easier for you, it may be easier to export the data yourself, so why not do that? It may be that the Cypher based export isn't detailed enough, or the structure the data is given in requires too much alteration to be useful by using Curl directly. These problems could be solved by exporting the data yourself, using a small script. Since you'll know what format you need your data in, it means it can be queried in the best way to fit the data. For example, if you know you only want nodes that have a particular label, then these can be targeted especially. The same also goes for the properties on these nodes, and also the relationships. Any part of the export can be tailored to meet the needs of the application using it.

This approach does mean additional time, as the export tool will need to be created, but it also means this tool will be tailored to its particular application, and that the export would be repeatable. This means there won't be the hassle of worrying about the process of exporting data from Neo4j anymore, as you'll have already built the functionality. When the time comes that a new project requires its data exported, the knowledge from the first exporter can be used to help with the second. In some cases the exporter could simply be moved to another project and configured to work with that application with minimal effort.

Although this approach has a big up-front cost in building it in terms of the time taken, the export process only needs to meet your needs, and that's it. This means the tool could be completely terminal driven to save on building a user interface, or if it did have one, it could be very basic in design. All the process has to do is export data in the write format, the other factors only become important if other people are going to see the export tool.

Summary

In this chapter we've been through how to handle your data within Neo4j via importing and exporting data. Whether you're starting a new project and are batch importing some data, or you're importing data from a previous project, we've been through it. Then after it's all in, we've also covered how to get your data out of Neo4j as well as how to back up the database.

When you're importing data, the CSV file is really important, and we've been over a few ways to ensure your CSV is valid before importing it, which saves headaches and unexpected errors later and always helps.

Importing data can be a pain, but knowing you can create an update query within Cypher that will create or update nodes as needed, as well as being able to create relationships makes it easier. If you have to run an import multiple times, sometimes with new data, sometimes with updated rows, that's all covered.

Of course you aren't always importing data, so exporting has also been covered. Sadly, Neo4j isn't the most equipped when it comes to exporting data, but you can still get your data exported, and that's the important thing. You'll also always have the option of exporting small datasets via the Browser, so if you ever need a quick export, don't forget the Browser is your friend.

Now that data moving in and out of the database has been covered, it's time to cover how to use data to create recommendations, calculate distances, and more. That's exactly what the next chapter is about. Now it's time to see the power Neo4j has to offer as we move into Chapter 7, Using data in Neo4j.

■ ■ ■

Querying Data in Neo4j with Cypher

When you've spent the time building up a data structure, planning the best relationships for the different node types, and of course collecting the data, you want results. Cypher allows us to take all of the hard work in building up a good dataset, and use that to give a better experience for users, or supply accurate recommendations. There are a lot of ways to analyze your data to show trends and gain insight into those that supplied it. Whether that is from a user making orders to generate more accurate recommendations on an e-commerce website or to a blog user seeing their most popular posts by seeing which of them has the most comments. There are many uses for data, and we're going to cover how to use Cypher to get the data you need for a multitude of situations.

To best showcase the wide range of Cypher's capabilities, there will be two main examples used. The first, will be a Pokémon-based example, composed of user-submitted data. The second, will be a location-based example, composed of generated data based on various locations. These two approaches demonstrate how Cypher can do both recommendation-based queries and distance-based ones as well. Both of these examples demonstrate the power of Cypher, and these can be adapted to various situations, including e-commerce, which will also be covered. The e-commerce application is an obvious choice for demonstrating recommendations, so aspects of the logic applied in the Pokémon example will also be applied to e-commerce.

With that out of the way, it's best to just dive right in to the Pokémon example, to demonstrate how Cypher be used to generate recommendations, and of course, the e-commerce application.

Recommendations, Thanks to Pokémon Data

I wanted to find an interesting way to generate data for use in the book and decided to get the community involved in supplying data. To as many people involved as possible, I decided to try and widen my audience, and make it something that would apply to anybody; anybody that liked Pokémon, that is. I'm a big fan of Pokémon, and figured I'd try to involve that, plus I know I'm not the only person who likes it. The idea of the application came from the original Pokémon slogan, *Gotta catch em' all!* Why not make that the objective? With the idea in place, I had to then build a website to make it happen.

Getting the Data, the Website Used

After seeing the slogan, it seemed a good idea to make a game out of catching them all, so that's just what happened. The idea was, you'd get one shot to randomly catch them all, but you could pick four Pokémon to reserve, so you could make sure you had your favorite. There were a couple of rules when it came to choosing these reserved Pokémon, but I'll get to those in a moment. While they were playing the game, it made sense to try to get some information about the user, which could be used when analyzing the data. The data recorded was picked for a reason, and all kept optional (most of the time, but we'll get to that) so it was all fair. This essentially meant that each user or Trainer (as they were labeled in Neo4j) that submitted data would get a random sample of Pokémon, ranging between 1 and 200. In addition to that sample, they would also have four Pokémon they'd reserved, and if they'd submitted it, some other personal information to go with this sample. As far as the user was concerned though, they'd just pick four Pokémon, fill in a form, then be presented with a page of Pokémon they'd caught.

The Pokémon that could actually be caught were the first 151, so there's a chance to catch Mew, as Mew is the 151st Pokémon, and was added after the initial release, for those that are interested, that is. That means that there is an actual chance to get all 151, as you get can get over 151 chances, and you already pick 4 to begin with.

Data Being Gathered

Of course I wanted to make sure the website was fun, but I still wanted to gather data that could be analyzed and was of course above all else, useful. Although supplying the data is entirely optional, each user had the option to submit the following information, supplied in Table 7-1.

Table 7-1. *The personal data recorded for those who submitted on pokemon.chrisdkemper.co.uk for use in the book and the reasoning for each*

Data item	Reasoning
Nickname	This was the best means of identifying a user if they wanted to be mentioned in the book.
Email	The e-mail address here was only used to contact those who were mentioned, just to let them know their nickname would be used (or not, as it seems).
Gender	There were only four Pokémon selected by the user, but gender is still a good value to have when it comes to analyzing data.
Age	Having an age for the user allows some nice range-based queries depending on the range of the data available, so again, it is useful to have.

Each item of data recorded had its own benefit, and of course is only used for this chapter. The e-mail data stored has since been removed, as the only reason it was needed was to contact those who've been featured in the book, and in a couple of cases, when they weren't, spam is always a problem, even if you use a reCAPTCHA.

Keeping the Spam Under Control

To try to keep spam users down to a minimum, I implemented a reCAPTCHA on the website, which is Google's offering in the fight against spam. If you've never come across one, it's just a checkbox you need to check if you're human, and it may also ask you to identify some similar images. Although technically spam data would just be anonymous data, I wanted to avoid 100% of the data being spam. If I'd wanted automated data, I'd have just scripted that.

The other advantage of the reCAPTCHA application means that although there will be anonymous data, it's still user-submitted anonymous data. This means, that the Pokémon characters that have been reserved, have all been picked by an actual person, provided the reCAPTCHA has been keeping the spam bots at bay.

Keeping the spam bots at bay was a priority, but I also didn't want to use completely anonymous data, because as I said earlier, I could have generated that. To get around this, I put in a validation check to ensure there wasn't more than 50% anonymous submissions already in the database.

If a user posted without a nickname, and 50% of the existing entries were anonymous, then they had to add a nickname to submit their data. They could still have anything as a username, nothing was unique, just as long as it was populated. The idea was that having another look at the form may allow for some additional data to be added, rather than the now required, nickname.

I used Cypher to pull out two figures to help with the calculation, the total submissions, and the number of anonymous submissions. The query used to achieve this is as follows.

```
MATCH (t:Trainer)
MATCH (a:Trainer {nickname: 'anonymous'})
RETURN count(DISTINCT t) AS total, count(DISTINCT a) AS anon;
```

The main thing to note in the above query is the use of DISTINCT, which ensures each node is only counted once, otherwise you run into a duplication problem. This duplication problem comes from count using both match statements to do the count, even though it shouldn't. Thanks to the multiple matches, this results in the same result for both values. To show this, first will be Figure 7-1, which will be the results without DISTINCT, and then Figure 7-2 soon after, show the results with DISTINCT.

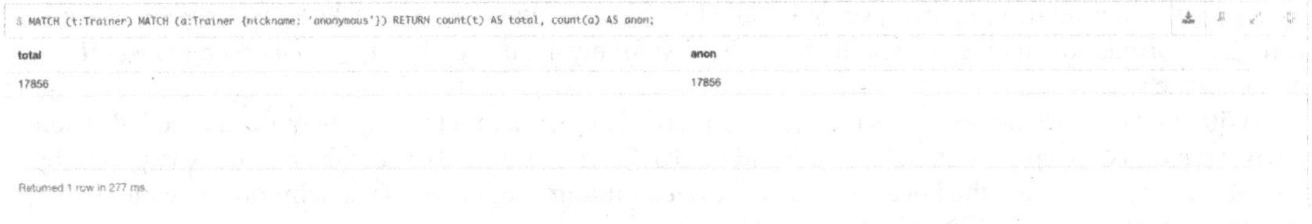

$ MATCH (t:Trainer) MATCH (a:Trainer {nickname: 'anonymous'}) RETURN count(t) AS total, count(a) AS anon;	
total	anon
17856	17856

Returned 1 row in 277 ms.

Figure 7-1. Showing the results of the Cypher query being used without DISTINCT

You can see in Figure 7-2 that the results are the same for both values, which is of course useless to us. To make this data actually useful, DISTINCT is added as shown in Figure 7-2.

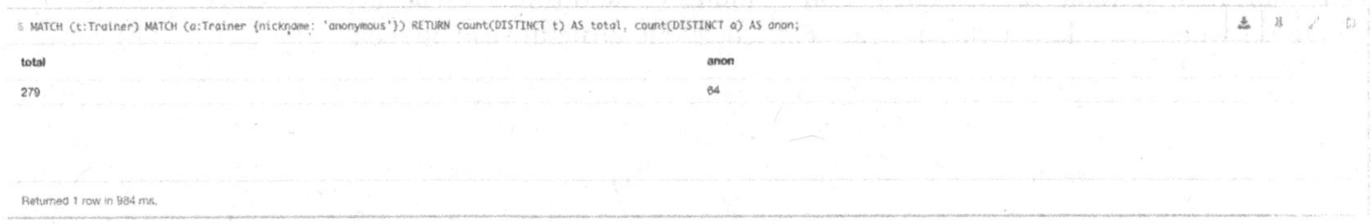

$ MATCH (t:Trainer) MATCH (a:Trainer {nickname: 'anonymous'}) RETURN count(DISTINCT t) AS total, count(DISTINCT a) AS anon;	
total	anon
279	84

Returned 1 row in 984 ms.

Figure 7-2. Showing the results of the Cypher query with the use of DISTINCT

You can see here there are now unique values being returned for each, which is much more useful. The interesting thing here are the values being returned. The first value was 6076 for both `total` and `anon`, and the actual values were 98 and 82, for `total` and `anon` respectively. The two unique values multiplied together: 98 * 62 equals the first value, 6076. This gives some reasoning behind the initial value, but also shows the importance of DISTINCT, in the times it's needed.

With the Cypher side out of the way, after the values are returned, they're used to work out a percentage, and if it's over 50%, the user cannot submit anonymously. If this user submitted data anonymously, with an unrounded percentage of 63.2, they'd have to add a nickname to get their shot at catching them all.

How the Data is Structured

To best understand how the queries work, you must first know the data you are querying against. In this case, all 151 Pokémon were imported into the database, with various different properties. An example of Bulbasaur, the first Pokémon (in terms of Id number, 1, that is) can be seen in Table 7-2.

Table 7-2. Bulbasaur's properties within the database

Property	Value
Name	Bulbasaur
Index	1
Height	7
Weight	69
Type	[poison, grass]

The data for each Pokémon was obtained from the Pokeapi, available at http://pokeapi.co. I wrote a script to import the Pokémon into Neo4j, based on the Id numbers, and then picked these properties to use. The API has a lot available to use, so it's worth looking at if you're doing a Pokémon-related project. The type(s) I wanted to store as an array, so they could be used as a filter later. The Pokeapi was a bit too verbose with the information it had regarding the types, at least for my needs, so I had to trim it down to just the names of the types.

With the Pokémon nodes, it was then just a case of relating a Trainer to the Pokémon as needed. There are two relationship types used, RESERVED and CAUGHT. The former, are the Pokémon that are picked by the user, and the latter, are the Pokémon that have been randomly assigned. This helps do some interesting queries later, including the most reserved Pokémon.

When a user submits their data, a Trainer node is created, with any information they supply attached as properties to the node. The Trainer is then related to their RESERVED Pokémon, with a RESERVED relationship, and the website assigns the CAUGHT relationships as needed. This database is one that is relationship heavy, as one user can have up to a maximum of 204 relationships, provided they get the highest achievable random value. An example of how a Trainer's relationships will be displayed can be seen in Figure 7-3, where a random node has been selected, and its structure can be seen.

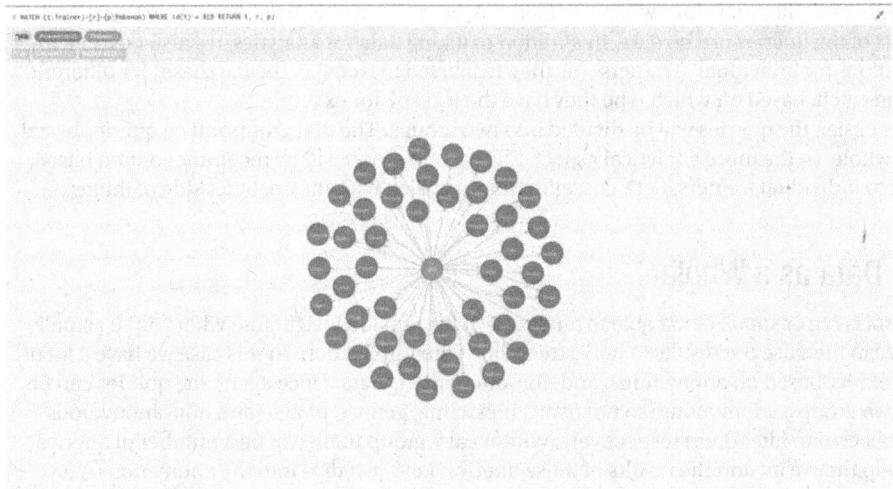

Figure 7-3. *The structure of Trainer node in the database, in this case node 919*

As you can see, Figure 7-3 shows that one Trainer has many relationships to Pokémon, in this case 54, to 48 different Pokémon. The query used to achieve this was as follows:

```
MATCH (t:Trainer)-[r]-(p:Pokemon)
WHERE id(t) = 919
RETURN t, r, p;
```

The query is just a normal relationship-based query, with a WHERE clause to filter it down to the trainer with the node id of 919. This example node shows how the relationships will work within the application, so when we get to the Cypher queries, the use of Pokémon and Trainer Labels will make a little more sense.

Rules for Choosing Pokémon

To make things a little bit more interesting there was a catch when it came to selecting which Pokémon you were allowed to pick. The first rule was that you were only allowed one starter Pokémon, or any evolution of that Pokémon. If you've ever played the games, you'll know that you only get a choice of one of three starter Pokémon, so this rule was to bring some of those feelings back. To give some extra choice, I allowed the inclusion of evolutions of the Pokémon, so you could pick Charmander, or Charizard for your starter, if you even wanted to pick one.

This rule means that it's possible to see the most popular starter Pokémon, including their evolutions, which is interesting for analysis. There was a similar rule applied for Fossil-based Pokémon, and also Legendary Pokémon for their uniqueness. The rules don't have any real impact on the process, it just allows for additional analytics points. When the actual Pokémon are picked by the system, these rules don't apply, so it's a 1/151 chance to get any particular Pokémon.

Querying the Data

With all the data collected (at the last point it could be before printing) it's now possible to use that data and work out a lot of different things. Although this dataset is mostly random, a lot can be learned from it, as the concepts used here can be applied to other things where the data won't be so random, such as e-commerce. A number of different values will be worked out, with the Cypher used to retrieve them, and of course, the results of the queries on the data. In addition to taking data for analytics, it's also possible to make recommendations for individual `Trainers` (as they're labeled in Neo4j in the database) for different Pokémon they could catch, based on which type they have the least of, for example.

To make things easier, the queries will be divided into two groups. The first group will be queries based on the dataset as a whole, so the more analytical aspect. The second group will be recommendation based, and will be applied to individual trainers. Let's get right into it, starting with the analytics side of things.

Analyzing the Data as a Whole

Whether your dataset is big or small, being able to analyze it helps provide insight into what you're actually collecting, and you can then use the results to help streamline your application. In this case we have a lot of random sets of Pokémon, based on anonymous, and non-anonymous data. Once again, the queries can be broken down into two groups, anonymous (so not using, nickname, gender, or age) and non-anonymous (using the values collected to filter data) respectively. Within each group there will be a number of queries based upon the group they're in, and the results of those queries. Let's just dive into the anonymous data sample, and do some queries on all of the data.

Anonymous Data Queries

These queries are ones that applied to the dataset as a whole, without taking any of the properties of the Trainer nodes (data submitted, along with their reserved Pokémon) into account. The first query will be totaling which Pokémon was the most popular overall, so let's get to it.

Most Popular Pokémon

In terms of trainers there are two kinds of Pokémon in the database, those they caught by means of them being randomly generated, and those they reserved. For this query, we don't care, we just want to know which is the most popular Pokémon between the Trainers, which in Cypher terms, is like this:

```
MATCH (:Trainer)--(p:Pokemon)
RETURN p.name AS name, count(p.name) AS count
ORDER BY count DESC
LIMIT 10
```

This query then gives the results seen in Figure 7-4.

name	count
Blastoise	228
Charizard	224
Pidgeot	219
Wigglytuff	216
Ninetales	215
Venusaur	215
Mewtwo	214
Alakazam	214
Nidoking	213
Kakuna	213

Figure 7-4. The first 10 results of the most popular Pokémon query

We'll get to the results in a minute, but the query itself isn't too complicated. First, we need the Pokémon that a Trainer has caught. We could have achieved this by using ()-[]-(p:Pokemon) which gets any Trainer to Pokémon, regardless of direction or type. This does work, but being specific in Cypher queries is always good for performance, and specifying the Trainer label helps speed up the query, even if only marginally. Since the relationship isn't considered here, that can also be dropped from the query, resulting in (:Trainer)--(p:Pokemon) being used.

After returning the data, it's time to arrange it in descending order, which is achieved with ORDER BY count DESC. Rather than getting all of the data, it's better to get a small subset, which in this case, was 15.

The Results

It's not surprising to see all of the top-level Pokémon in the list. Although these results are random at this stage, it's still good to see. That's enough about those, let's move on to more specific queries.

Who Caught the Most

Since the website was based around catching them all, finding out if anybody did is a big deal, so let's get started on the query. What we essentially need to see here is which trainers got the most relationships, but only unique relationships, to remove the duplicates. This is achieved with the following Cypher query:

```
MATCH (t:Trainer)--(p:Pokemon)
RETURN id(t) AS id, t.nickname AS name, count(DISTINCT p.name) AS count
ORDER BY count desc
LIMIT 10
```

Using this query, the following results were obtained, which can be seen in Figure 7-5.

id	name	count
306	KeV	118
333	Jonnyboy	115
412	anonymous	115
400	anonymous	115
310	veonik	113
403	anonymous	113
287	figr0ll	112
297	Zephsace	112
381	anonymous	112
185	Arc	110

Returned 10 rows in 357 ms.

5 MATCH (t:Trainer)--(p:Pokemon) RETURN id(t) AS id, t.nickname AS name, count(DISTINCT p.name) AS count ORDER BY count desc LIMIT 10

Figure 7-5. *The results of the query showing which users caught the most Pokémon*

This query is a little difficult, and the most important part is the use of the id function. The match here gets the Trainers that have caught Pokémon, regardless of their type, as we want them all. Next the data is just returned, with DISTINCT p.name being counted. Without the id function in the query, this count would actually make all of the values of 't.name` unique, and then sum the corresponding values. This means that rather than multiple anonymous values, there would be one super anonymous value, with all of the various count totals added to it. The id function then ensures each node is evaluated individually, in this case keeping the duplicates.

The Results

It was user `KeV` that managed to get the top spot here. Sadly there wasn't a score of 151, but I'm sure, given enough shots, somebody would get it eventually. If you invert this query, it reveals that the lowest score was a tie between CJ, schlocke, and hill79 all had a tie at 5. That's unlucky, I blame Team Rocket.

Most Popular CAUGHT and RESERVED Pokémon

We've already seen the results for the most popular Pokémon, but we've yet to see the values for the specific types. In this case, we'll be covering the most popular randomly caught Pokémon. This really provides insight into how the balance was between the different numbers, so essentially if it was actually fair. The query isn't too different from the previous one, it just has a small change. The full query is as follows:

```
MATCH (:Trainer)-[r:CAUGHT]-(p:Pokemon)
WITH count(p.name) AS total_count
MATCH (:Trainer)-[r:CAUGHT]-(p:Pokemon)
WITH p.index AS id, p.name AS name, count(p.name) AS total, total_count
RETURN id, name, total, total_count AS `Total Caught`
ORDER BY total DESC
LIMIT 10
```

With this query, you then get the results seen in Figure 7-6.

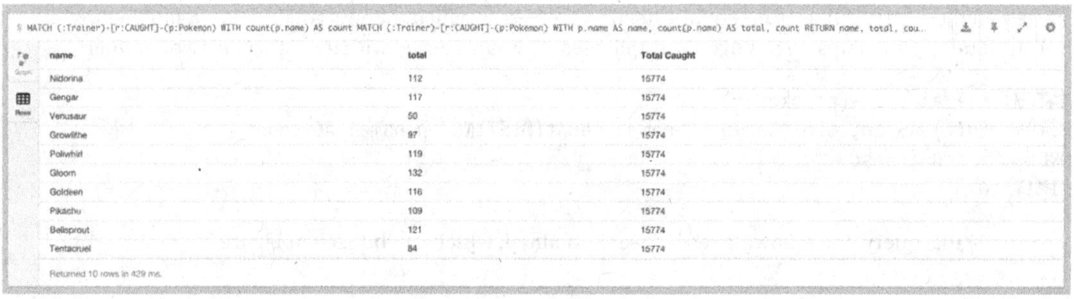
$ MATCH (:Trainer)-[r:CAUGHT]-(p:Pokemon) WITH count(p.name) AS count MATCH (:Trainer)-[r:CAUGHT]-(p:Pokemon) WITH p.name AS name, count(p.name) AS total, count RETURN name, total, cou...

name	total	Total Caught
Nidorina	112	15774
Gengar	117	15774
Venusaur	50	15774
Growlithe	97	15774
Poliwhirl	119	15774
Gloom	132	15774
Goldeen	116	15774
Pikachu	109	15774
Bellsprout	121	15774
Tentacruel	84	15774

Returned 10 rows in 429 ms.

Figure 7-6. *Shows all of the CAUGHT Pokémon, with an included total*

The query used to generate these results is a little different from the previous ones, as it has multiple MATCH statements. The first MATCH statement is to get the total number of CAUGHT Pokémon within the database, which could be used to work out the percentage of the total each Pokémon has. This value could have been obtained from its own query of course, but this way it's included on every result row, so if it's needed it's there.

To ensure both queries work as expected, WITH is utilized, to help only pass the relevant information to the rest of the query. You can see that the count of `p.name` has been aliased to `count` using AS. In the next statement, another WITH is used, which essentially just passes these values to the RETURN clause, so they can be returned. When using WITH, you'll see that the `count` from the first statement is also included in the WITH of the second. Without this inclusion, `count` would not be defined for use in the return statement.

Another thing to mention about the first query is the value it returns. If you ran that query by itself, it would be like so:

```
MATCH (:Trainer)-[r:CAUGHT]-(p:Pokemon)
RETURN count(p.name) AS `Total Caught`
```

Since only a count is returned, and nothing node related, then all of the values that would be returned if the count was specific to the node (just like in the second part of the previous query) are added together, and returned as one total value. The rest of the query just gets some additional information about the Pokémon being returned, and also orders the results by the most counted, in descending order.

Given how the relationships are set up within the database, determining the most popular RESERVED Pokémon, rather than the most random CAUGHT Pokémon requires one change, the relationship type. The modified query can be seen below.

```
MATCH (:Trainer)-[r:RESERVED]-(p:Pokemon)
WITH count(p.name) AS total_count
MATCH (:Trainer)-[r:RESERVED]-(p:Pokemon)
WITH p.name AS name, count(p.name) AS total, total_count
RETURN name, total, total_count AS `Total Reserved`
ORDER BY total DESC
LIMIT 10
```

Depending on the use case, it may be possible to remove total count from the query as we're looking at this data as user-selected data, so whomever is on top is the most popular. That being said, having the total allows us to work out the percentage of the total each value was, so whether or not this query can be trimmed down can be decided. The modified query gives the results seen in Figure 7-7.

5 MATCH (:Trainer)-[r:RESERVED]-(p:Pokemon) WITH count(p.name) AS total_count MATCH (:Trainer)-[r:RESERVED]-(p:Pokemon) WITH p.name AS name, count(p.name) AS total, total_count RETURN...		
name	total	Total Reserved
Charizard	47	1093
Blastoise	40	1093
Mewtwo	35	1093
Dragonite	33	1093
Arcanine	31	1093
Pikachu	27	1093
Zapdos	27	1093
Gengar	26	1093
Alakazam	25	1093
Venusaur	24	1093
Returned 10 rows in 190 ms.		

Figure 7-7. *The results of the most popular RESERVED Pokémon query*

Most Popular Pokémon Type

Each Pokémon has at least one type within the database; in some cases, two. These values have been stored in Neo4j as an array of string values, which means they can be used within queries, provided the values are treated the same as they are stored, so in this case, strings. The query now needs to take the types from all of the caught Pokémon, and ensure the list is ordered by the most popular type. That's enough talk, let's get straight into it. The Cypher for the query can be seen below.

```
MATCH (:Trainer)--(p:Pokemon)
WITH p.type AS types
UNWIND types AS type
RETURN type, count(type) AS total
ORDER BY total DESC
LIMIT 10
```

As we're only interested in Pokémon data, the Trainer alias can be left off as it's not used. The interesting part of the query comes with the use of UNWIND, which allows each individual type to be counted, rather than treating multiple values as one row. If the above has been run without the UNWIND, then any time a Pokémon had more than one type, this combination would be counted as one type, rather than two different types.

We already know Bulbasaur's types from previously in the chapter, which are poison and grass. Without the use of UNWIND, the combination of poison and grass would be counted as one value. Essentially, the use of UNWIND allows each item in the array to be evaluated as an individual item.

Thanks to the combination of WITH and UNWIND, it means that when the data has to be counted, it's already just a huge list of types, so they just need to be counted, ordered, and of course the type itself needs to be returned, so the numbers make sense. This query gives the result shown in Figure 7-8.

```
$ MATCH (:Trainer)--(p:Pokemon) WITH p.type AS types UNWIND types AS type RETURN type, count(type) AS total ORDER BY total DESC LIMIT 10
```

type	total
poison	6043
water	5780
normal	3882
flying	3501
grass	2672
psychic	2575
ground	2512
bug	2220
fire	2204
rock	2037

Returned 10 rows in 509 ms.

Figure 7-8. *The results of the query to determine the most popular types within the database*

This query could be modified slightly to give more specific result sets depending on the use case, so if you wanted to know the most popular type within RESERVED Pokémon, just add a relationship constraint to the query. It could be also possible to see what is the most popular type among the Pokémon, regardless of the Trainer input, which would look like so:

```
MATCH (p:Pokemon) WITH p.type AS types UNWIND types AS type
RETURN type, count(type) AS total
ORDER BY total DESC
LIMIT 10
```

This allows you to see which are the most and least popular Pokémon types, so if you wanted to catch specific types to strengthen your team, that could be done using this query. The only real change in this query is the removal of the Trainer relationship, as we can just query the Pokémon nodes directly to get the types in this case. Speaking of the results of the Trainer version of the query, let's go through those.

Non-Anonymous Data Queries

All of the previous queries have been based on completely anonymous results, but the database isn't all anonymous, so it's time to look at what data we have available. As mentioned earlier, the fields recorded were `nickname`, `gender`, `email`, and `age`. Really, out of these fields, there are only two that can be of any real use, which are `gender` and `age`. With these fields, it allows the data to be categorized by age ranges, and of course, gender.

Of course, had I collected more data, such as location, there would have been more granular results, but with age and gender values, this still gives some values. We'll be performing a number of queries using these values to help filter down the results, and give some insight into those that submitted their data to be used.

Popular Pokémon Filtered by Gender

We've already done a query to work out the most popular Pokémon, so with a couple of alterations, it can be modified to return gender-specific values. The resulting Cypher query can be seen below.

```
MATCH (t:Trainer)--(p:Pokemon)
WHERE t.gender = 'male'
RETURN p.name AS name, count(p.name) AS count
ORDER BY count DESC
LIMIT 10
```

In this query, we need to use the values of the Trainer node, so `t` has to be in to supply data for the filter. In terms of the stored data, the gender property will be either set to `male`, or `female`, or be null, as it only gets set if there's a value to set. In the WHERE, it'll remove null values by default, unless specified otherwise. Since we don't want the null values, then the basic WHERE does the job. To get the female results it's just a case of swapping out `male` for `female` in the query. You can see the results of this query in Figure 7-9.

$ MATCH (t:Trainer)--(p:Pokemon) WHERE t.gender = 'male' RETURN p.name AS name, count(p.name) AS count ORDER BY count DESC LIMIT 10

name	count
Nidoking	128
Blastoise	123
Charizard	120
Weepinbell	117
Paras	116
Venusaur	114
Wigglytuff	113
Pikachu	113
Jolteon	113
Mewtwo	111

Returned 10 rows in 168 ms.

Figure 7-9. *The results of most popular Pokémon query, filtered by gender, in this case `male`*

Switching the results to filter by `female` rather than `male` gives the results, seen in Figure 7-10.

$ MATCH (t:Trainer)--(p:Pokemon) WHERE t.gender = 'female' RETURN p.name AS name, count(p.name) AS count ORDER BY count DESC LIMIT 10

name	count
Weedle	40
Mewtwo	39
Pidgeot	39
Ninetales	38
Pidgey	38
Charmander	38
Poliwhirl	38
Eevee	37
Poliwag	37
Wartortle	36

Returned 10 rows in 172 ms.

Figure 7-10. *The results of most popular Pokémon query, filtered by gender, in this case `female`*

Popular Pokémon Filtered by Age

Having access to age is a brilliant way to filter data, as it allows you to filter by age ranges, as well as an individual age. If you want to filter by an age range, you can either have these preset, or decide them based on what values are available within your data. In this case, we'll be checking the ages submitted, and using those values to build up acceptable ranges on which to base the main query. First, we need all the ages that have been submitted and the counts for these, which in Cypher terms looks like this:

```
MATCH (t:Trainer)
RETURN t.age AS age, count(t.age) AS count
ORDER BY count DESC
```

In addition to giving the different range of ages within the data, it also gives the most popular, which although it's not particularly useful in this case, being able to identify your key age or age group is always a good thing. To get this value, the query just needs to be ordered by the `count`, rather than the `age`. The results of the query can be seen in Figure 7-11.

```
MATCH (t:Trainer) RETURN t.age AS age, count(t.age) AS count ORDER BY count DESC LIMIT 10
```

age	count
25	20
21	15
22	14
26	13
24	12
23	12
19	11
18	10
20	10
30	5

Returned 10 rows in 83 ms.

Figure 7-11. *A query to show all of the submitted ages within the database*

With a slight modification it could also be possible to use an age range with the query, which would look like so:

```
MATCH (t:Trainer)--(p:Pokemon)
WHERE t.age > 18 AND t.age < 21
RETURN p.name AS name, count(p.name) AS count, t.nickname
ORDER BY count DESC
```

Recommendation-Based Queries

After covering queries that were based on the data as a whole, it's time to get to a more personal level and recommend different things to the Trainers. Each Trainer node has at least 4 relationships to different Pokémon within the system, which means there are still 147 different choices available. Unless you're like Ash (the main character in Pokémon) and want to 'Catch them all', you may want to apply some strategy to the Pokémon you catch. This is where the recommendations come in.

Recommend Pokémon, Based on Type

As a trainer, it would be nice to know what types you have the most of, because this shows you which areas you may need to build on. Even if that's of no use to you, knowing which areas you are weakest in could be, so let's get to working that out, shall we? A node id used previously was 919, so we'll use it again here. Trainer 919 needs the types of all of the Pokémon they have caught, and the counts for them.

```
MATCH (t:Trainer)-[]-(p:Pokemon)
WHERE id(t) = 919
UNWIND p.type AS type
RETURN type, count(type) AS total
ORDER BY total ASC
```

With the query in place, Trainer 919 gets the results seen in Figure 7-12. In this query, we're selecting Trainer 919 using WHERE id(t) = 919 after getting all of the Pokémon related to said Trainer. Since the type is an array, it needs to be iterated, which is where UNWIND comes in. After that `type`, and the count of `type` are returned. Thanks to count aggregating the `type` values to count them, it also removes the duplicates from the rows, which is useful in this case.

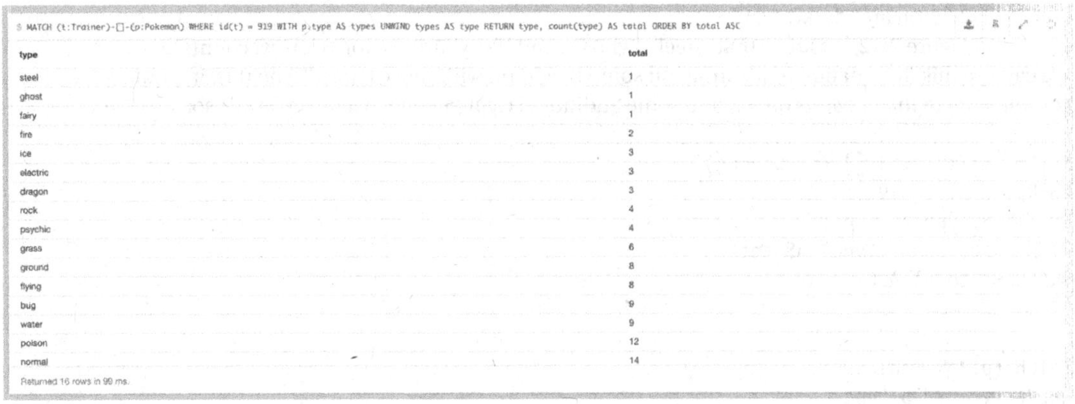

type	total
steel	1
ghost	1
fairy	1
fire	2
ice	3
electric	3
dragon	3
rock	4
psychic	4
grass	6
ground	8
flying	8
bug	9
water	9
poison	12
normal	14

Query: `$ MATCH (t:Trainer)-[]-(p:Pokemon) WHERE id(t) = 919 WITH p.type AS types UNWIND types AS type RETURN type, count(type) AS total ORDER BY total ASC`

Returned 16 rows in 99 ms.

Figure 7-12. *The types and their counts for the Pokémon Trainer 919 has*

The only bad thing about this list is there are no zero values, so what if Trainer 919 doesn't have a type at all? Well, there's an easy way to check, we just need to get all of the different types that the Pokémon have, look at the total. Using Cypher, that looks like this:

```
MATCH (p:Pokemon)
UNWIND p.type AS type
RETURN DISTINCT type
```

This query gives the results seen in Figure 7-13. This query is a slimmed down version of the one used above. In this case, because the count is being used in the return, duplicate values will be returned, so to get around that, DISTINCT is used.

Figure 7-13. The results of a query to get a unique list of all the Pokémon types

With that query, we find that there are 17 types returned, and Trainer 919 only has 16, so we know there's one missing. There should technically be 18 types, there is one missing, which is the `dark` type. It is not included in the list because it wasn't introduced until the second generation, and therefore none of the first 151 Pokémon are `dark`.

From Figure 7-12, we know that `steel`, `ghost`, and `fairy` are the top 3 lowest counts, at 1 each. We can use this information to recommend some Pokémon with those types. To do this, it requires the combination of the previous query, and some additional Cypher code, which looks like so:

```
MATCH (t:Trainer)-[]-(p:Pokemon)
WHERE id(t) = 919
UNWIND p.type AS type
WITH type, count(type) AS total, t
ORDER BY total ASC
LIMIT 3

MATCH (p:Pokemon)
WHERE type IN p.type
AND NOT (t)--(p)
RETURN p.name, p.type
LIMIT 5
```

The first part of the query is the exact one from before, just with a WITH clause in place of RETURN. The values passed over by WITH have already been evaluated, so type is being iterated over, and counted. With the use of WITH, each of the types from the previous query can be used in WHERE. Since the types are stored in an array, they must be filtered using IN, as you cannot compare two arrays. This essentially means to compare two arrays, you must be first iterating over the first, then use IN to check if the value is in the second.

In this case, the query is checking to see if one of the top 3 types (`steel`, `ghost`, and `fairy`) are within a Pokémon's type array. There's nothing worse than being recommended something that you already have, and the same goes here. To get around this, AND is used to add that the Trainer cannot be related to the Pokémon returned. Gotta catch em' all, right? To stop too many choices being returned, the results are limited, after the `name` and `type` are returned. The results of the query can be seen in Figure 7-14.

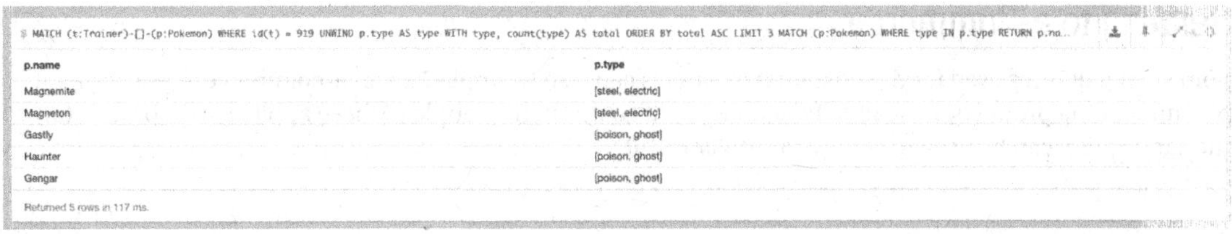

Figure 7-14. *The top 5 results for Pokémon with the least popular types that Trainer 191 had*

This data can be incredibly useful for Trainer 919 to help them catch some Pokémon that round out their types a little better. If this information was fed back into the Pokémon website, it should easily recommend these Pokémon as good suggestions to catch. The ordering of the query could also be reversed to show a list of Pokémon that should be caught to add to the more popular types owned, which would help if you were trying to get all Pokémon of a certain type, for example.

What's Left to Catch

If you're attempting any kind of collection, it's always nice to have an idea of how much is remaining, and a Pokémon Trailer is no different. It's always handy to have a list of the renamed Pokémon you had to catch, and luckily Cypher can help with that using the following simple query.

```
MATCH (p:Pokemon), (t:Trainer)
WHERE id(t) = 919
AND NOT (t)--(p)
RETURN p.name
```

Once again we use Trainer 919 as an example by using the combination of WHERE and the id function. We're also matching Pokémon (`p`), but without any matches this time. Essentially what's being done here is any Pokémon that aren't related to Trainer 919 are then returned, and we have our list of remaining Pokémon. The results for this query can be seen in Figure 7-15.

Figure 7-15. *The remaining Pokémon Trainer 919 has to catch*

Relating to e-Commerce

Some of the queries used for the Pokémon examples can also be applied to an e-commerce application for recommending products, instead of Pokémon. We'll go through a couple of these applications to show how the same query can be used to achieve a similar result.

Most Popular Product

Knowing which product is the most popular in your store is always going to be a good thing. We've already calculated the most popular Pokémon caught by Trainers, which is essentially customers buying products. In an e-commerce based structure, products would be somehow related to customers, either directly, or through orders. This link allows you to query the dataset for any products that have a customer or order connection, and then count those. This will give stats on the most popular products, which could then be broken down by category. Assuming that orders were related to products in some way, an example Cypher query would look like so:

```
MATCH (p:Product)--(:Order)
RETURN p.name AS name, count(p.name) AS count
ORDER BY count DESC
LIMIT 15
```

Since a product is related to an order, provided the relationship exists, it has been bought. With this match in place, it's just a case of returning the product name, with a count of the products, and finally ordering by that count, in descending order. This particular query has a limit of 15, but this could easily be changed to say 1, to only return the top product.

This same logic, applied on a per-customer basis, would allow you to see which products your customers bought most often. You could then take these products, and promote deals containing them, or the products themselves to the customer, because you know these are deals they'll be interested in. Assuming the same structure as before, but with the addition of a customer being related to an order, an example Cypher query would be like so:

```
MATCH (p:Product)--(:Order)--(c:Customer)
WHERE id(c) = 919
RETURN p.name AS name, count(p.name) AS count
ORDER BY count DESC
LIMIT 15
```

The same query as before now adds another relationship to the match, in the form of a `Customer` node. When a customer makes an order, their node will be related to an order node, which will be related to product nodes. This gives the customer a link to the products, which query takes advantage of using a WHERE to filter the results. This gives the customer the most purchased products, and can be then used to promote any deals containing those products.

Most Popular Product Category

A customer may buy a whole range of products, but only ever buy each one once. If you were to try to work out their most popular product, there wouldn't be much information to go on. The products themselves though will be part of a category, and it may be that this customer likes a particular category. Depending on how the categories have been set up, it may be that each product has an array of categories, much like our Pokémon nodes and their types. The same query used for getting the most popular type can also be used here for the most popular category. However, the more likely case will be that products are related to categories via Category nodes, which would contain many products.

If the categories are related as nodes, then it then means you can access a customer's favorite category through the products they've bought. This can be achieved building on the query used in the previous example, and would look something like this:

```
MATCH (c:Category)--(:Product)--(:Order)--(u:Customer)
WHERE id(u) = 919
RETURN c.name AS name, count(c.name) AS count
ORDER BY count DESC
LIMIT 15
```

The query adds another relationship to the MATCH clause, including the Category nodes that are related the purchased products of the customer. In this case, the WHERE and the customer relationship could be removed, which would give an overall view on the most popular products within the whole store.

Recommended Products

Just as we recommended Pokémon to Trainers earlier, it's just as easy to recommend products to customers. Depending on your use case, you may want to recommend a customer's most popular product to them or just those in the same category. In the case of the category, there isn't too much that needs to be added to the previous query, used to get the top categories. All that's required is to get the products related to the linked categories, which would look something like this:

```
MATCH (p:Product)--(c:Category)--(:Product)--(o:Order)--(u:Customer)
WHERE id(u) = 919
AND NOT (o)--(p)
RETURN p.name AS name
```

The query gets the products from the related categories, but in the AND, also checks to make sure the product and order nodes are not related, as this would mean the products have been purchased before. Of course, this would just return products in the same category, but there may be other values available to make the query more accurate, and therefore give more targeted results.

Thank You

Before moving on, I have to thank all of those who participated in the Pokémon website, and submitted their data to be used in the book. I may never meet any of the users who submitted data to the website, but I can at least thank each and every person for submitting their data and helping make this chapter. As I mentioned earlier, I wanted to make this chapter a little different, and thanks to the community that has happened.

The project itself will be available on GitHub when the book is published (with the data removed, of course) so anyone can look at the code. As the url isn't known yet, if you're interested in seeing the project, just check my github account, chrisdkemper and look for it there.

Location-Based Queries

Out of the box, Neo4j doesn't handle location-based queries, but with the addition of a plugin, that can easily be changed. The plugin in question here is the Neo4j Spatial plugin (https://github.com/neo4j-contrib/spatial) which adds location-based functionality to Neo4j. Although we won't be detailing all of the functionality included in the plugin here, if you'd like to find out more then have a look at the github page.

To do these queries there are a couple of steps you need to take to allow for the data to be used. For now though, these steps won't be covered (as they will be in the next chapter) so these queries assume you've got the spatial plugin setup for them to work.

For now we need an example. Where I live, Newcastle, UK, there is a local rail system called the Metro. I've gathered the location data for these rail lines so it can be used in the examples. Within the region there are 60 stations, so for these examples it'll be using various random points within the city, and around the stations in question. This should give an idea on how to perform the queries needed to return nodes based on location, that can be adapted to your own application.

Figure 7-16 shows how the data looks in the browser if you run MATCH (n) RETURN n on the Metro station database, with the spatial database set up.

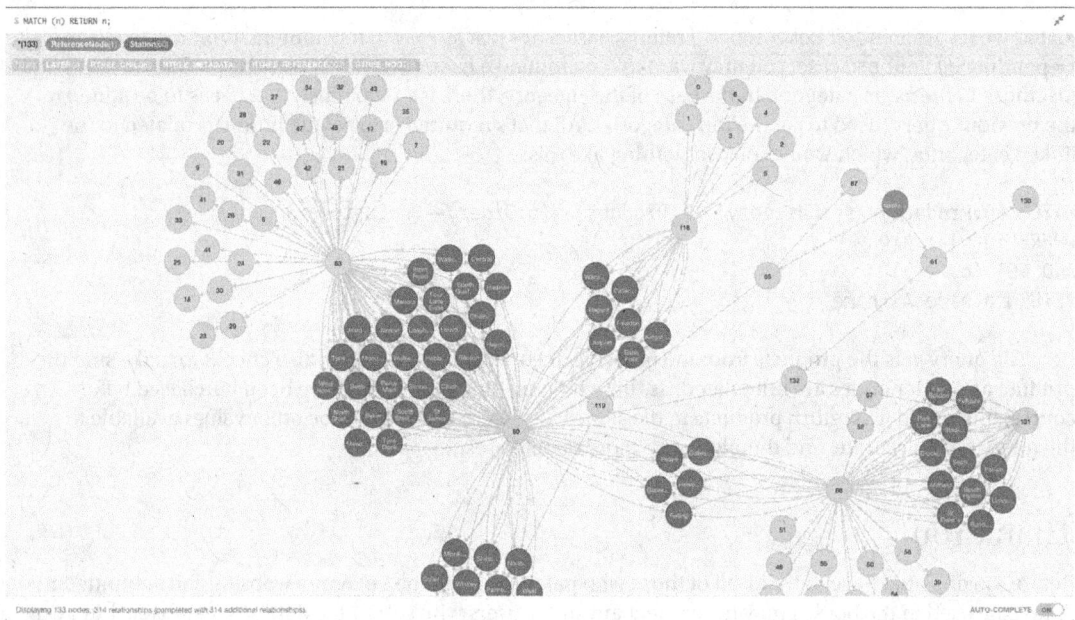

Figure 7-16. *The result of running MATCH (n) RETURN n; on a database location data set up on the spatial plugin*

You can see the stations with various relationships linking groups of stations. You'll have to take my word for the fact that the areas that have the most relationships are where the stations are the closest together. This helps give an idea of how the spatial plugin works. With that out of the way, let's look at some queries, starting with where the closest Metro station is.

Closest Metro Station

If you're in a strange place, being able to find the closest mode of transport could always be useful, so we'll do that here, just with Metro stations. The cypher needed to achieve this query isn't too complicated, we just need a location and a distance. The distance needed is in kilometers, and a location to start from is provided. When this is queried in Cypher, it's looked up via the plugin and the results are returned, and can be used as needed in your application. In this case, the query is where the nearest Metro station is. The query needed to run this query is as follows:

```
START n=node:geom("withinDistance:[54.9773781,-1.6123878,10.0]") RETURN n LIMIT 1
```

The location being used here is one near City Hall. If you run this query the result can be seen in Figure 7-17. The query itself is using START to initiate a traversal of the graph. It then uses the geom index to perform the function, which has arguments of latitude, longitude, and distance (in kilometers) respectively.

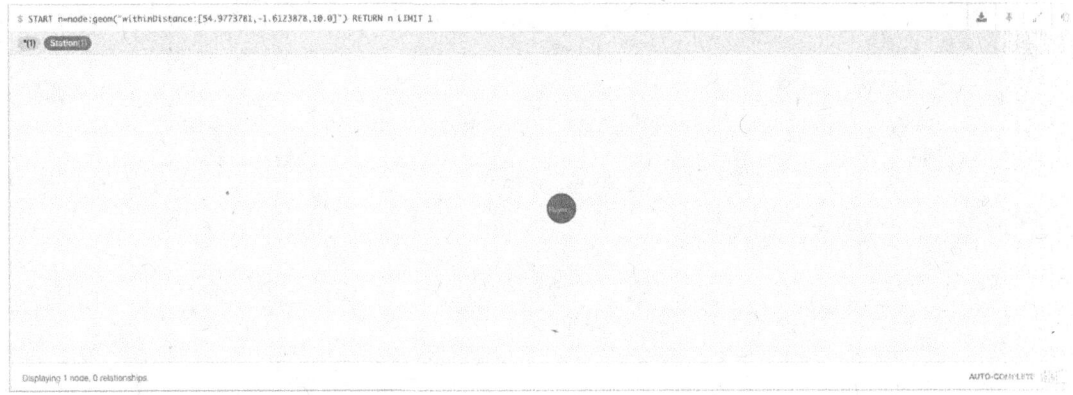

Figure 7-17. *The result of performing the distance query for a given location on Metro station data*

You'll just have to take my word on the fact that the query is correct as Haymarket is in fact the closest Metro station to that location at City Hall. This shows how easy it is to query located data, so with a bit of setup (which will be covered in the next chapter), you'll be able to have location awareness in your applications.

Summary

Through the course of the chapter, a large spectrum of different query types have been shown and demonstrated, using (hopefully) interesting means. There's been many different types of recommendation and analysis queries from the Pokémon website, and the closest location query made possible by the spatial plugin. These varying uses will hopefully be useful enough to help push you in the right direction when it comes to your own applications. Now though, it's time to build an application that takes everything we've done so far in the book and puts it all together.

■ ■ ■

CHAPTER 8

Building an Application with Neo4j

It's time to put Neo4j to use in a proper application, and in this chapter we'll be doing just that. We'll be going from setting up the location plugin, right up to how to use it in location queries. The application will be in the form of a location app. To cover any location-based copyright issues, we're going to base ourselves in Antarctica for this chapter. Although it may not be feasible to have a travel system like one being built here in Antarctica, it's a big wide-open space that allows for the locations to be added. To begin with, we'll be going with busses (which I'll get to in a minute) as a transport system and adding some bus stops to the system.

To make things easier I've written some commands to take care of importing data into the application, so when you go through the code (which will be available on github) you'll be able to add your own sample data as well. The commands in place (that will be explained individually as needed) are to import Bus Stops for a small sample location, which will be built on as the chapter progresses.

In the application, Cypher will be used wherever possible when communicating with Neo4j. This means that if you'd like to apply the same logic in your own application, then the Cypher query used is available for you to use.

A Quick Note on Code Comments

To ensure the example site always works, changes may need to be done to the example site to keep it up and running. When performing these changes, code samples used in the chapter may no longer make sense, or may no longer exist in the new application. Since there's a chance of this happening, any code sample will include a PHP comment, an example of which can be seen below:

```
/**Sample:CodeSample01**/
```

The comment will always have "Sample:" before it, then an ID after. Using this system, if you're referencing a sample in the chapter, search for the sample value and if it changes locations or gets modified, the comment will also be moved. If this does happen, an explanation of why will be there, so any changes can be made accordingly. The changes will be available via github (https://github.com/chrisdkemper/sample-neo4j-php-application) as well, so the commit history will also be available. The code on github is a Vagrant box, which contains the environment required to run the website, so all you'll need to do is run `vagrant up` and Vagrant will do all of the hard work for you.

With that out of the way, it's time to get into setting up the application, which starts with setting up the location plugin.

Installing the Spatial Plugin

Before you can do location-based queries you need to have the spatial plugin installed and ready to use. The code available from github will install the plugin as part of the provisioning process, but the instructions will be covered either way. To begin with, you need to get the plugin, which is available at: https://github.com/neo4j-contrib/spatial. The project offers many ways to install the plugin, but the easiest is to use one of the pre-built archives. The archive needed is named based on the Neo4j version, so get whichever one you need, in this case it's the one for 2.3.0.

The process of installing the plugin will be similar regardless of the system Neo4j runs on (stop the server, install the plugin, etc.), but in this case the instructions for an Ubuntu server will be used. If you aren't running Ubuntu, then your plugins directory will be located wherever you've installed Neo4j. With the archive downloaded, you then need to stop Neo4j from running, which can be done like so:

```
service neo4j-service stop
```

Once the service is stopped, the archive needs to be unzipped in the plugins directory (which is /var/lib/neo4j/plugins on Ubuntu) so that the .jar files sit within the plugins directory. The archive can be unzipped by using the following command, which may need to be installed (with apt-get if your system doesn't have it: apt-get install unzip)

```
unzip /vagrant/neo4j-spatial-XXXX-server-plugin.zip -d /var/lib/neo4j/plugins
```

In this example, the path and name would need to be modified to meet your needs, but the basic command is there. If you're able to unarchive the directory another way, moving the .jar files can be done like so:

```
mv /vagrant/neo4j-spatial/*.jar /var/lib/neo4j/plugins
```

With the plugin files in place, it's time to start Neo4j again which is done with the following command:

```
service neo4j-service start
```

That's it. With Neo4j running again the Spatial plugin is now running and ready to be used.

Setting up the spatial index

With the plugin installed, the next step is to create a spatial index to utilize it. This needs to be done for the queries to work, and also for the nodes to be found by Cypher. To create the index, the following JSON needs to be posted to the endpoint http://localhost:7474/db/data/ext/SpatialPlugin/graphdb/addSimplePointLayer

```
{
        "layer":"geom",
        "lat":"lat",
        "lon":"lon"
}
```

In this JSON, you can see the keys "lat" and "lon" which in this case, have the same as values. The values to those keys needs to be what you're calling your latitude and longitude properties on your nodes. This ensures the correct data is collected from the nodes added to the index. The value for "layer" is "geom", which is the name of the layer. This can be replaced with another name if you require, but make sure the name used is consistent for all steps, or it won't work. If you were to change the name of the index, in the following examples just replace "geom" with your choice of name.

The next index that needs to be added is for Cypher, and requires data to be posted to
`http://localhost:7474/db/data/index/node/` and also has another requirement. To allow this to work,
the nodes that will be in the index need to have an id field that matches their node id. This can be done by
using a query like the following:

```
MATCH (n) WHERE id(n) = 0 SET n.id = id(n) RETURN n
```

You would of course need to change 0 for whichever node id you wanted to update, but this would allow
the node to be given the property. This could also be done with a label if required for mass updates, which
would be achieved using the following code for a Place label:

```
MATCH (n:Place) WHERE id(n) = 0 SET n.id = id(n) RETURN n
```

With the nodes given their id property (by whichever means) the index needs to be created, but posting
the following JSON to the previously mentioned URL.

```
{
        "name":"geom",
        "config":{
                "provider":"spatial",
                "geometry_type":"point",
                "lat":"lat",
                "lon":"lon"
        }
}
```

This index allows Cypher to be able to communicate with the spatial index, allowing the queries to be
possible. With the indexes in place, that's pretty much it. The next step is to then add nodes to the index so
they can be queried. This is achieved by sending a POST request to `http://localhost:7474/db/data/ext/`
`SpatialPlugin/graphdb/addNodeToLayer`, with the following JSON:

```
{
        "layer":"geom",
        "node":"http://localhost:7474/db/data/node/0"
}
```

The layer is kept as "geom" as it has been throughout the example, and the other value needed is the
node. The value here is the url of the node in the database, which (when it isn't escaped) looks like so
`http://localhost:7474/db/data/node/0` with 0 being the id of the node.

Those are all the steps needed to get up and running with the spatial plugin, but as mentioned, the
creation of these has been added into commands so they don't need to be run on this system.

What the App is Being Built On

The website application itself will be built on PHP, using the Silex micro-framework. Before we go any
further, it's worth mentioning that you don't need to know PHP for these examples, it just happens to
be my language of choice and isn't required for Neo4j. For those who aren't familiar with PHP, you may
notice in that the opening PHP tag (<?php) isn't closed in some cases. For files that contain only PHP, it's
recommended to omit the closing tag for various reasons, so that's why it's missing. For its comments, // can

be used for a single line comment, but can equally be started with /* and ended with */. You'll see examples of both in this chapter, and also in the application itself, so if you weren't aware of what PHP comments were before, you know now.

With that out of the way, it's time to talk a little about Silex, the framework being used to build the application. Siliex is a framework inspired by Sinatra (built on Symfony2 and Pimple), so if you are familiar with Sinatra/Flask/Expressjs/SparkJava/Scalatra/etc. these examples may feel familiar.

There will be some samples of PHP, but this will be explained where required. There are a number of commands that have been created to add sample data, so these will be run. With the data available to query, it'll then be time to start doing some Cypher queries.

How the Data will be Structured

Breaking down how the data is structured is better done by the different labels of the data, so with this in mind, the headings for the different labels can be found below.

Place/BusStop

Each of the locations in the application are classed as "Place" nodes, which contain the location information. These places will also have names, so they can be identified by other processes. With any given place, if there is, for example, a bus stop, then a node of that type ("BusStop" in this case) will be related to it. This means if a location has many transport options, it'll keep relationships down.

Timetable

To allow for the journey planning aspect of the application, the timetables will hold a lot of the power. A timetable will be related to any of the "Place" nodes it has on its route with the STOP_ON_JOURNEY relationship. On this relationship, there will be a property of time with the value (in minutes) of how far along the journey that "Place" is. This allows the application to use these values to calculate travel time, but also keeps the hops been different "Places" small. The data being related in this way means that if different timetables connect two different places, then the trip can still be planned.

The timetable itself will also have a name, and will store a list of the days, and also the times it runs. This means that if the same route is used multiple times, it saves on duplication. This also provides the ability to use the times for journey planning purposes.

Transport

The transport node is the mode of transport being used and has a name and a type. For example, for a bus, you could use a name of "A1" with the type of "bus". The transport node then relates to any timetables it uses with the RUNS_ON relationship.

Building the Application

The application itself will be built using PHP, and hosted on a local web server powered by Nginx. This is then wrapped in an ubuntu server, which is provided via a Vagrant box. Rather than just all custom PHP a micro framework called Silex will be used to make some of the base operations easier, such as URL routing and template management. Silex will essentially be used to glue all of the different aspects of the application together, which will be discussed a little later in the chapter.

To give a better overview on the application itself, Figure 8-1 shows how the files within the src directory are laid out, which is where the majority of the code lives.

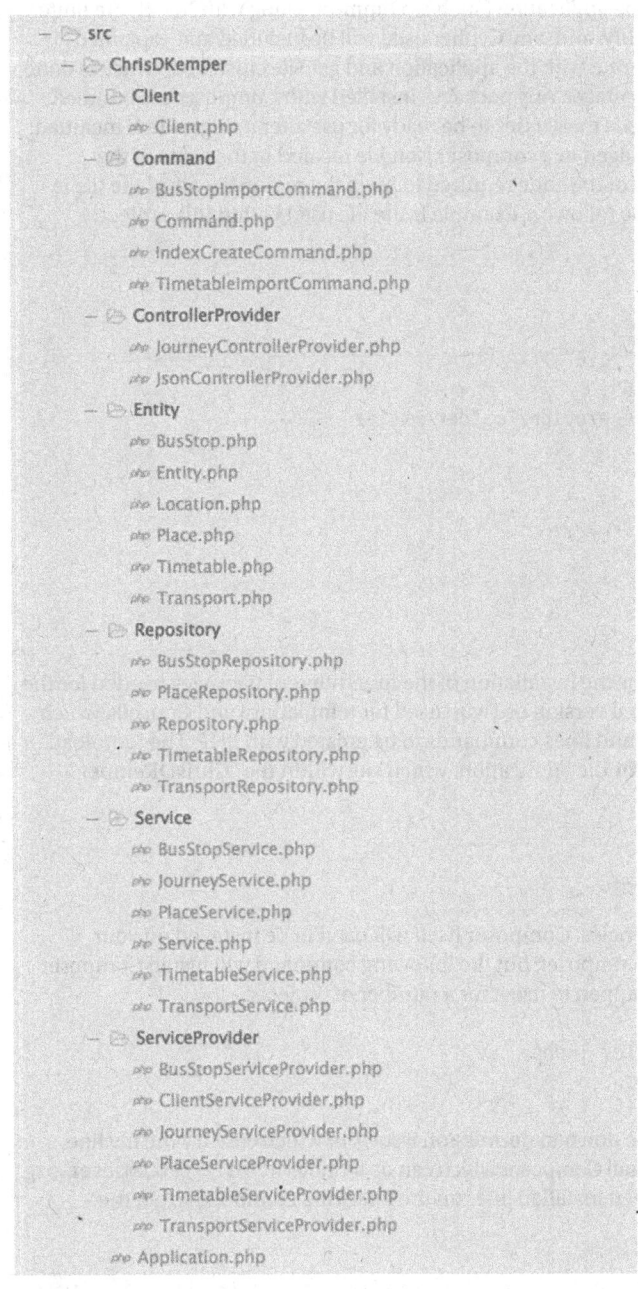

Figure 8-1. *The src directory of the application*

Each of the folders are named based on what they contain, but those aspects will be covered a little later. Since this is a book on Neo4j, and not on PHP, I won't be going into too much detail about how all of the different aspects of the application work. In these cases, all you need to be aware of is that the code does what is described and it all works. Some aspects of the application (such as communicating with Neo4j) are quite important and will be explained more thoroughly, and, any Cypher used will be included and explained.

With that out of the way, it's time to get started with the application and get Silex installed, which is done via the use of Composer, a PHP dependency manager. Any packages installed with Composer are bundled together in an autoloader, which essentially loads the classes to be ready for use after a single file is included.

The dependencies for Composer are managed in a composer.json file located in the route of the application directory. This then downloads all of the code required to meet the requirements of the file is downloaded into a directory called vendor. The following example is the file used within this project:

```
{
        "require" : {
                "silex/silex": "~1.2",
                "symfony/twig-bridge": "~2.6",
                "symfony/console": "~2.6",
                "knplabs/console-service-provider": "dev-master"
        },
        "autoload": {
                "psr-0": {
                        "ChrisDKemper": "src/"
                }
        }
}
```

The "require" portion of the JSON contains the installation of the four different packages needed for the application. Included in the list are the extended version of Twig (used for templating) and Console, which is a symfony component that allows for command lines commands to be created with PHP. The "autoload" component loads in the custom code written for the application, which sits within the "ChrisDKemper" namespace.

Installing Composer

Since were using Composer to install dependencies, Composer itself will need to be installed on your system. There are a number of ways to install Composer, but the following command will install Composer global on your system, which is useful if you happen to use it for a number of projects.

```
curl -sS https://getcomposer.org/installer | php
mv composer.phar /usr/local/bin/composer
```

If the above command fails, then it may be down to permission issues, in which case try the mv line preceded with sudo. There are other ways to install Composer which can be found at https://getcomposer.org, the Composer website. After Composer has been installed just run the following command to get the dependencies installed

```
composer install
```

Once Composer has finished doing its work you'll be ready to go.

Setting Up Silex

A default Silex application would be initiated with the following code, which would be in the index.php file located in the web directory of your server, or whichever folder your web server uses. It'll be broken up in the different lines, then shown as a whole.

```
require_once __DIR__.'/../vendor/autoload.php';
```

The first thing to note in this file is the inclusion of autoload.php, which is how the autoloader created by Composer is made available to the application.

```
$app = new Silex\Application();
```

The main Silex application is loaded here, and assigned to the $app variable which allows for its functionality to be accessed.

```
$app->get('/', function() use($app) {
    return 'Hello';
});
```

This is an example of a route within Silex which in this case is a GET route for '/', that returns the string 'Hello' when accessed. The second parameter of the function, after the route (/) is the callback function, which is followed by use. The use of use allows for the $app variable to be available within the function, because without the use, $app would be out of scope, so to allow it to be used, it's passed in with use. Although this is a GET route (signified by $app->get), you can have different route types to meet your needs, for this application there will be use of both GET and POST requests.

```
$app->run();
```

The application is executed last in the file and any routes or functionality added before this point will be available when the file is served from the server. This all comes together to form the following file:

```php
<?php
require_once __DIR__.'/../vendor/autoload.php';

$app = new Silex\Application();

$app->get('/', function() use($app) {
    return 'Hello';
});

$app->run();
```

All of this together in a file called index.php would show 'Hello' on the screen.

Silex Service Providers

To make adding features easier to Silex it offers the ability to register Service Providers, which allow for chunks of functionality to be added at the same time. In the application, these are used to add functionality required for the different entity types, which are essentially the different node labels that were previously mentioned. Service Providers are also used to add set features, such as implementing templating.

Creating the Index.php File

Although a basic example of Silex has been covered, it's not the one used in this application. The file itself is quite similar, which can be seen below:

```
$app = require __DIR__ . '/../app/bootstrap.php';
$app->run();
/**Sample:Index.php**/
```

To keep the bootstrapping of the application away from running it, the $app variable is now created from the contents of the bootstrap.php file. This file contains all of the main functionality of the application, including any routes used, as well anything else required for the website to run. Like the Silex example, the file will be broken up into sections and explained to give an overview of the functionality offered by the application.

```
require_once __DIR__.'/../vendor/autoload.php';

$app = new ChrisDKemper\Application(array('debug' => true));
```

This segment is the same as the Silex example in the sense that it's creating the main application, but in this case an extended version of the application is created instead. This application class sits within the ChrisDKemper namespace, and allows for the application to be tweaked when it's created. The extended application adds the templating functionality to Silex and also adds the ability for service providers to be used.

```
/*
 * Register the client to communicate with Neo4j
 */
$app->register(new ChrisDKemper\ServiceProvider\ClientServiceProvider(), array(
    'client.username'   => 'neo4j',
    'client.password'   => 'password',
    'client.transport'  => 'localhost',
    'client.port'       => 7474,
    'client.https'      => false
));
```

The first service provider is for the Client class, which is how the application communicates with Neo4j. Details required by the client are supplied here, allowing them to be easily updated, should the environment the application is hosted on change. The functionality of the Client class will be explained in more detail a little later, but the ClientServiceProvider added to Silex here simply makes the functionality of the class available to the rest of the application.

```
/*
 * Register the console application
 */
$app->register(new Knp\Provider\ConsoleServiceProvider(), array(
    'console.name'              => 'App',
    'console.version'           => '1.0.0',
    'console.project_directory' => __DIR__.'/..'
));
```

The ConsoleServiceProvider is a third party service provider which is used to enable the Symfony Console component for use within the application. It grants the ability to create terminal commands to be written with PHP, which is utilized to create various helper commands for the website.

```
/*
 * Register the Place service provider
 */
$app->register(new ChrisDKemper\ServiceProvider\PlaceServiceProvider());

/*
 * Register the BusStop service provider
 */
$app->register(new ChrisDKemper\ServiceProvider\BusStopServiceProvider());

/*
 * Register the Timetable service provider
 */
$app->register(new ChrisDKemper\ServiceProvider\TimetableServiceProvider());

/*
 * Register the Transport service provider
 */
$app->register(new ChrisDKemper\ServiceProvider\TransportServiceProvider());
```

Here we have service providers, which add a Repository and a Service for a different node type, sharing the name of the service provider. Having the different node types separated off makes it easier to get, for example, all of the Place nodes within the site, as you'd just query the Place service. Each of these different node types work in the same way, with the exception of the Place service, which has some additional functionality. How the Services and Repositories work, and how they're put together will be covered in more detail later, but these service providers add that functionality to Silex.

```
/*
 * Since the homepage is static, pointless putting it in a provider
 */
$app->get('/', function () use ($app) {
    return $app['twig']->render('index.twig');
});

/*
 * Journey routes
 */
$app->mount('/journey', new ChrisDKemper\ControllerProvider\JourneyControllerProvider());

return $app;
```

The final code segment is responsible for registering the routes used within the application. The first of which is the same as the basic Silex example, but rather than returning 'Hello' it returns a Twig template. The other routes are supplied by the JourneyControllerProvider which is a collection of the different routes. Each of the routes within the provider are mounted on '/journey' meaning that will proceed any of the specified routes. For example, a '/plan' route exists within it, and to access that particular route, you would need to use the URL '/journey/plan'. With the controllers added, the application is then returned for use in the index. php file.

Communicating with Neo4j

Although there are a lot of different Neo4j clients available to use, for the sake of the book I opted to use curl commands and Cypher. This gives the code the most re-usability regardless of the platform, as all that needs to change is how the curl request is done. Rather than using large curl command blocks, a number of different functions have been created to make certain actions within the site easier, and as with the other examples, will be broken up into sections and explained. The file in question is located at /src/ChrisDKemper/Client/Client. php (based on the layout of the code within the repository) and started as follows:

```php
<?php namespace ChrisDKemper\Client;

class Client
{
        protected $curl_headers = array();
        protected $base_url = 'http://localhost:7474';
        protected $cypher_uri = 'db/data/transaction/commit';
        protected $spatial_uri = 'db/data/ext/SpatialPlugin/graphdb/addSimplePointLayer';
        protected $index_uri = 'db/data/index/node/';
        protected $spatial_node_index = 'db/data/ext/SpatialPlugin/graphdb/addNodeToLayer';
```

First, the namespace of the file is set to help with the autoloading, then the class is declared, and it's followed by a number of protected properties for the class. The various properties with the _uri suffix are URLS needed to perform certain actions on Neo4j, such as creating indexes, or running Cypher queries

```php
public function __construct($username, $password, $transport = 'localhost', $port = 7474,
$https = false)
{
        /**Sample:Clientconstruct**/
        //Set the default headers
        $this->curl_headers = array(
                CURLOPT_CUSTOMREQUEST => "POST",
                CURLOPT_RETURNTRANSFER => true,
                CURLOPT_HTTPHEADER => array(
                                'Content-Type: application/json'
                        )
        );

        //Set the base_url
        $this->base_url = sprintf("%s://%s:%s",
                false == $https ? 'http' : 'https',
                $transport,
                $port
        );

        //Set auth header
        $this->curl_headers[CURLOPT_USERPWD] = sprintf("%s:%s", $username, $password);
}
```

This is the _construct function, which allows you to perform actions when the class is created. The data that has been passed through here was originally supplied in the bootstrap.php file, and is the information required to communicate with Neo4j. Each of the requests all share certain common headers, so to save on duplicated code, these are set in here in a way they can be shared throughout the class. One of the headers is the authentication header, which is created using the supplied username and password. In the construct function, the base url needed for the queries is constructed using any information supplied; otherwise it defaults to http://localhost:7474.

```php
public function cypher($cypher_query)
{
        /**Sample:Cyphermethod**/
        //Set up a statement for the transaction
        $data = array(
                        'statements' => array(
                                array('statement' => $cypher_query)
                        )
                );

                //Use the preset cypher uri to send the query
        return $this->send($this->cypher_uri, $data);
}
```

The previous code is the cypher method within the client class, which is used a lot throughout the application. This method allows for cypher queries to be easily done by only taking the cypher query as an argument. It then sets up the required code needed to run a Cypher statement, and then passes that to a base send method, which actually makes the request. The layout for the Cypher transaction is the same as in previous examples.

```php
public function createSpatialIndex($name = "geom", $lat = "lat", $lon  = "lon")
{
        /**Sample:createSpatialIndex**/
        //Set up a statement for the transaction
        $data = array(
                "layer" => $name,
                "lat"   => $lat,
                "lon"   => $lon
            );

                //Use the preset cypher URI to send the query
        return $this->send($this->spatial_uri, $data);
}
```

There we have a function to help create a spatial index on the Neo4j instance. The method takes three arguments: layer name, lat, and lon. The layer name is as described, but the lat and lon values are to see what the longitude and latitude values properties are called on the node. The data is then set up in the correct format for the query, the URI, and payload of the function as passed to the send method, which makes the request and returns the response.

```php
public function createCypherIndexForSpatial($name = "geom", $lat = "lat", $lon = "lon")
{
        /**Sample:createCypherIndexForSpatial**/
        $data = array(
                        "name" => $name,
                        "config" => array(
                                "provider" => "spatial",
```

```
                                    "geometry_type" => "point",
                        "lat"       => $lat,
                        "lon"       => $lon
                    )
        );

            return $this->send($this->index_uri, $data);
}
```

To allow for the spatial index to be queryable by Cypher, another index needs to be created. To make this easier it's been made into a method on the client that takes a name, lat and lon as an argument. These details need to match that of the spatial index that has previously been created, so the defaults here reflect the same default values as the method used to create the spatial index. Like that method, the data for the query is formatted correctly, then passed to the share send method to perform the query, then the result is returned.

```
public function spatialAddNodeToLayer($name, $node)
{
        /**Sample:spatialAddNodeToLayer**/
        $data = array(
                        'layer' => $name,
                        'node'  => $node,
                );

            return $this->send($this->spatial_node_index, $data);
}
```

When applicable nodes are created (the ones with location information) they must be added to the spatial index so they can be queried, which requires sending a request to the spatial plugin. Like the other commands, this command sets up the data required to accomplish this action, then passes it to the send method with the correct url. The data needed here is the name of the layer that the node is being added to, and also the Neo4j URL for the node.

```
public function getBaseUrl()
{
        return $this->base_url;
}
```

This is a small method to get the base url used for the queries. Although the base url is stored as a variable, it cannot be accessed outside of the class directly, therefore if it's needed outside of the class, it either needs to be public, or have a method to return it. In this case, I've opted for the method to return it.

```
protected function send($uri, $data)
{
        /**Sample:clientSend**/
        $data_string = json_encode($data);

        $url = $this->base_url . "/" . $uri;
        $query = curl_init($url);
```

```
//Add the post data to the query
$this->curl_headers[CURLOPT_HTTPHEADER][] = 'Content-Length: ' . strlen($data_string);

//Add the headers to the query
foreach($this->curl_headers as $header => $value)
{
        curl_setopt($query, $header, $value);
}

curl_setopt($query, CURLOPT_POSTFIELDS, $data_string);

$result = curl_exec($query);
        curl_close($query);

        return json_decode($result, true);
}
}
```

This is the main method within the client, as it's the one that actually performs the queries. To avoid code duplication, a shared method was used which allows for the more specific commands to pass in the URL they need the request to be sent to, and the data to send. Since the rest of the queries are structured the same (same headers, authentication, etc.) it makes sense to use a shared function. The first thing that happens is that the supplied data is then converted to JSON to be sent to Neo4j, as that is the required format for it. The next few lines of code pull in the default headers to the curl request (that were set when the Client class was created), as well as setting the necessary headers for posting data via curl. With the headers set up, the request is then executed, curl is closed, and the decoded JSON output is returned to whichever function has called it.

Using the Client

Now that the client has been explained, it's time to go into how it's actually used. The main communication between the application and Neo4j are done using Repositories and Services. The client is passed into the repository, to allow the repository to communicate with Neo4j, and then various methods are exposed to make getting data out of Neo4j easier. The repositories just interact with Neo4j and don't apply any real business logic, and this is where the Services come in. A Service will take a repository as an argument, so it can get the required information from Neo4j, then apply any required changes to make it suitable for use within the application. This means that when you want to get some data for a particular type of node, such as BusStop, then you get that data by using the BusStop service, which in turn calls the BusStop repository, which then asks Neo4j for the data via the Client.

Since the Repositories are the main place that communication between Neo4j and the application take place, it makes sense to run through them to see how they work. They are all set up using extension, where there is a base repository that does all of the work, and that repository is extended to customize for the different types, should this be required. In this case the repositories that extend the base aren't very complex at all, and all follow the same pattern, which we will cover in the moment.

Below we have the Repository file (/src/ChrisDKemper/Repository/Repository.php broken up into sections and explained as needed.

```php
<?php namespace ChrisDKemper\Repository;

use
    ChrisDKemper\Client\Client
;

/**
* The base repository
*/
class Repository
{
        protected
                $client,
                $label = ''
        ;

        public function __construct(Client $client)
        {
                $this->client = $client;
        {
```

In this class we first see the namespace declaration, followed by the inclusion of the client class via use. Using use just means that rather than going 'new ChrisDKemper\Client\Client', 'new Client' can be used. The client is already built before the repository is created, so it's then assigned to the client property within the class. There is also a label property, which is blank. This is how the extended repositories work, they simply change this label value which then changes the nodes that will be returned by the repository.

```php
public function create($properties)
{
        /**Sample:repositoryCreate**/
        $query_data = array();

        foreach($properties as $key => $value)
        {
                $value = is_string($value) ? sprintf('"%s"', $value) : $value;

                if(is_array($value)) {
                        if(is_numeric($value[0])) {
                                $value = sprintf('[%s]', implode(',', $value));
                        } else {
                                $value = sprintf('["%s"]', implode('", "', $value));
                        }
                }

                $query_data[] = sprintf('%s : ', $key) . $value;
        }

        $query_string = implode(", ", $query_data);
```

```
//Run the create query
$cypher = sprintf("CREATE (n:%s {%s}) RETURN id(n);", $this->getLabelQuery(),
$query_string);

$data = $this->client->cypher($cypher);

$id = $data['results'][0]['data'][0]['row'][0];

//Update the node to have a self referencing id
//Run the create query
$cypher = sprintf("MATCH (n) WHERE id(n) = %s SET n.id = id(n) RETURN n, id(n),
labels(n);", $id);

$data = $this->client->cypher($cypher);

$node = $data['results'][0]['data'][0]['row'][0];
$node['id'] = $data['results'][0]['data'][0]['row'][1];
$node['label'] = $data['results'][0]['data'][0]['row'][2];

return $node;
}
```

One of the main methods within the repository is the create method, which is used for creating nodes. The labels for the created nodes are taken from the label property within the repository, so if you extend it, then the nodes created will have that label. For example, the BusStop repository extends the base repository and has a label value of 'BusStop'.

An array of properties to be stored on the node are passed into the method. These are then iterated over and processed to be used within a cypher query. Since you need to supply, for example strings wrapped in quotes, you cannot handle each property value the same. The code in this method assumes all of the properties are correctly formatted. With the properties processed, this is then added to the cypher query, and creates a node with the label.

When the node is created, just the ID is returned. Another query is then run immediately after, to ensure the node has the `id` field required for the location plugin. The cypher used to set this id is as follows:

```
MATCH (n) WHERE id(n) = 0 SET n.id = id(n) RETURN n, id(n), labels(n);
```

In this case the code has been substituted again with an id of 0. In the code though, the ID is returned from the previous query so it can be used right away without any issue. This query also returns all of the information about the node so that it can be passed further down the application.

```
public function one($id)
{
        /**Sample:repositoryOne**/
        $query_string = sprintf("MATCH (n:%s) WHERE id(n) = %s RETURN n, id(n), labels(n);",
        $this->getLabelQuery(), $id);

                $data = $this->client->cypher($query_string);

                if(empty($data['results'][0]['data'])) {
                        return array();
                }
```

```
            $node = $data['results'][0]['data'][0]['row'][0];
            $node['id'] = $data['results'][0]['data'][0]['row'][1];
            $node['label'] = $data['results'][0]['data'][0]['row'][2];

            return $node;
}
```

This method is used to retrieve a node based on its Id, so if you just need a particular node, then it can be retrieved. As with the other queries in the repository, the label is also supplied to the Cypher query, which gives it that additional bit of filtering when it comes to retrieving the node. If the Id of the node is correct, but the label doesn't match then a node won't be returned. This essentially means that if you want to access a particular node type, this must be done from the specific repository. Either way, the query is done using the cypher method once again, and the data is formatted in a way that it will be usable by the rest of the application, and is then returned.

```
public function all()
{
        /**Sample:repositoryAll**/
                $query_string = sprintf("MATCH (n:%s) RETURN n, id(n), labels(n);",
                $this->getLabelQuery());

                $data = $this->client->cypher($query_string);

                $nodes = array();

                foreach($data['results'][0]['data'] as $row)
                {
                        $node = $row['row'][0];
                        $node['id'] = $row['row'][1];
                        $node['label'] = $row['row'][2];
                $nodes[] = $node;
                }

                return $nodes;
}
```

The all method is utilized when you'd like all of the nodes with a certain label to be returned. In the method, a basic MATCH query is performed which matches any nodes with the given label. Of course, in the base repository this would return all of the nodes, as no label exists, but in the repositories that extend this one, they'll have a label set, which allows the filter to work. Any applicable nodes are then processed and finally returned.

```
public function find($property, $value)
{
        /**Sample:repositoryFind**/
                if(empty($value)) {
                        return array();
                }
```

```php
        if(is_array($value)) {
                if(is_numeric($value[0])) {
                        $value_string = sprintf('IN [%s]', implode(' ,', $value));
                } else {
                        $value_string = sprintf('IN [\'%s\']', implode('\' ,\'',
                        $value));
                }
        } else {
                if(is_int($value)) {
                        $value_string = sprintf(' = %s', $value);
                } else {
                        $value_string = sprintf(' = \'%s\'', $value);
                }

        }

        $query_string = sprintf("MATCH (n:%s) WHERE n.%s %s RETURN n, id(n),
        labels(n);", $this->getLabelQuery(), $property, $value_string);

        $data = $this->client->cypher($query_string);

        if(empty($data['results'][0]['data'])) {
                return array();
        }

        $node = $data['results'][0]['data'][0]['row'][0];
        $node['id'] = $data['results'][0]['data'][0]['row'][1];
        $node['label'] = $data['results'][0]['data'][0]['row'][2];

        return $node;
}
```

Sometimes you need to make a node based on a property value, and this method allows that to happen. It takes a property name and a value as an argument, then does a query accordingly. Since properties can have many different types, a number of checks are done to ensure the data is formatted correctly. For example, if the data is an array, then it's covered for use with Cypher's IN clause. In addition to setting up the in, it also checks what the type of the first item in the array is. This is to ensure that if integers are passed in, they're supplied without quotes and that strings are supplied with quotes.

All of this processing is to ensure the WHERE clause of the query is formatted correctly. The resulting node is then built up from the result and returned.

```php
private function getLabelQuery()
        {
                return is_array($this->label) ? implode(":", $this->label) : $this->label;
        }
}
```

This method is a little helper method to format the labels in the correct way. If the label happens to be an array, then the label needs to be separated by a colon to work with Cypher, such as Label:Anotherlabel. To save on doing this check every time, it's placed into another method, so the change can be made in one place, rather than in every other method that uses it. If there is just a single label available in the repository, then this method will just return the label name.

Whole file here?

As mentioned, this repository does all of the work other than including the labels, so many different node types can be created without having to duplicate the functionality of the base repository. To show how little is done when extending the repository, the contents of the BusStopRepository.php (/src/ChrisDKemper/Repository/BusStopRepository.php) are as follows:

```php
<?php namespace ChrisDKemper\Repository;

/**
* The repository for BusStops
*/
class BusStopRepository extends Repository
{
        protected
        $label = 'BusStop'
        ;
}
```

The only code in the file, other than the object declaration is the setting of $label to 'BusStop'. This value is then used when accessing the methods of the base repository, so whether you're using the create or find methods, the value of $this->label will be 'BusStop'.

As previously mentioned, the repositories are not called directly, but instead are called via the service. These services call the specified repository under the hood, and then apply certain logic or formatting to the data before it is returned to the application. The services used to fetch nodes implement four methods: create, one, all, and find. These methods take the same arguments as the respective functions in the repository so allow for the same data to be retrieved. Once the data is retrieved via the repository, it's then formatted into arrays of entities, depending on the type of data being managed. For example, the BusStop service file (/src/ChrisDKemper/Service/BusStopService.php) contains the following:

```php
<?php namespace ChrisDKemper\Service;

use
        ChrisDKemper\Entity\BusStop
;

class BusStopService extends Service
{
        public function create($properties = array())
        {
                /**Sample:serviceBusStopCreate**/
                $node = $this->repository->create($properties);

                if($node) {
                        return new BusStop($node);
                }

                return false;
        }
```

The first method in the class is the create method, which (just like the repository) takes an array of properties as an argument. You'll see here that no processing is done of the properties, they're simply passed to the repository, where all of the actual work is done. The result is then saved to a variable, and if that variable isn't false a new BusStop is returned. This class represents the BusStop entity. The entities in this case are just empty classes that allow access to the properties that exist on a node. Whenever nodes are returned, the individual nodes are returned as an entity of the respective type, meaning properties can be accessed in the same way, no matter what the node type is.

```php
public function one($id)
{
        /**Sample:serviceBusStopOne**/
        $node = $this->repository->one($id);
        if($node) {
                return new BusStop($node);
        }

        return false;
}
```

Just like with the repository implementation of this method, the only argument is a node id. This is then used to query the underlying repository and return the result it comes back with (wrapped in a BusStop class, of course), provided said result isn't fault.

```php
public function find($property, $value)
{
        /**Sample:serviceBusStopFind**/
        $node = $this->repository->find($property, $value);

        if($node) {
                return new BusStop($node);
        }

        return false;
}
```

As with the previous methods, all of the work here is done within the repository and the property and value arguments are passed through to the repository. If there is a resulting node, then this is returned wrapped in the entity class.

```php
public function all()
{
        /**Sample:serviceBusStopAll**/
        $nodes = $this->repository->all();

        if(empty($nodes)) {
                return array();
        }

        $busstops = array();
```

```
        foreach ($nodes as $node)
        {
                $busstops[] = new BusStop($node);
        }

        return $busstops;
        }
}
```

The all service is probably the most basic service, as it simply just gets all of the nodes from the repository and puts them in a list, or returns an empty array if no nodes exist.

Each of the other node services work in the same way, the only difference being the name of the entity being returned from the methods, which in this case is BusStop. The Place service however does go against this pattern slightly, as it requires additional information that the other nodes don't. The reasoning for this is that Place nodes are very important in the application, as they're the ones that have all of the location information. Also, without any additional information, there'd be no way of knowing if a Place was a Bus Stop, or any other transport type, so some additional processing is required. The 'one', 'find', and 'create' methods are the same as the BusStop example, however the all method is as follows:

```
public function all()
{
        /**Sample:servicePlaceAll**/
        $nodes = $this->repository->all();

        if(empty($nodes)) {
                return array();
        }

        $places = array();

        foreach ($nodes as $node)
        {
                $place = new Place($node);
                $cypher = sprintf("MATCH (n)-[:LOCATED_AT]-(t) WHERE id(n) = %s RETURN
                labels(t)", $place->id);
                $data = $this->client->cypher($cypher);

                foreach($data['results'][0]['data'] as $row)
                {
                $label = $row['row'][0][0];

                if( ! in_array($label, $place->label)) {
                        $place->label[] = $label;
                }
                }

                $places[] = $place;
        }

        return $places;
}
```

The first half of this method functions the same as the others, as it gets all of the nodes from the repository. Rather than just retuning each node though, this code does some additional processing. The Cypher query that is performed is getting all of the labels of the related nodes that have the LOCATED_AT relationship with that particular place. This allows for different styling to be used on the frontend of the website, and gives some additional context on what different transport types a Place has access to.

There is one additional service that is used within the website which is the Journey service, which isn't tied to nodes like the others are. This service is used within the application to perform certain location-based queries easily, and its methods are as follows:

```
public function closestPlace($lat, $lon, $km = 5.0)
{
        /**Sample:serviceJourneyClosestPlace**/
        $cypher = sprintf('START n=node:geom("withinDistance:[%s,%s,%s]") RETURN n, id(n),
        labels(n)', $lat, $lon, $km);

        $data = $this->client->cypher($cypher);
        $row = $data['results'][0]['data'][0]['row'];

        $node = $row[0];
        $node['id'] = $row[1];
        $node = array_merge($node, $row[2]);
        $node['label'] = $row[3];
        $place = new Place($node);
        return $place;
}
```

Unlike the other services, this one has the Client passed in when it's created, allowing it to communicate with Neo4j directly. It also doesn't take a repository either. This uses Neo4j spatial to find the closest node within a given distance. Since only the Place nodes have location data, it can be assumed that any nodes returned will be places, so they can be returned in the correct entity wrapper.

```
public function closestTransport($lat, $lon, $km = 10.0, $type = '')
{
        /**Sample:serviceJourneyClosestTransport**/
        if( ! empty($type)) {
                $type = $type . ":";
        }

        $cypher = sprintf('START place=node:geom("withinDistance:[%s,%s,%s]") WITH place
        MATCH (place)-[:LOCATED_AT]-(transport%s) RETURN place, id(place), labels(place),
        transport, labels(transport) LIMIT 1', $lat, $lon, number_format($km, 1), $type);

        $data = $this->client->cypher($cypher);
        $row = $data['results'][0]['data'][0]['row'];
        $node = $row[0];

        $node = array_merge($node, $row[3]);
        $node['id'] = $row[1];
```

```
        $node['label'] = $row[4];
        $place = new Place($node);

        return $place;
}
```

The closestTransport method is an extended version of the closestPlace method, and is a little more complex. The Cypher query still looks for the closest node using the supplied information, but when this is found, it then uses WITH to get the nodes related with the LOCATED_AT relationship. The rest of the code then takes the data from both the returned place and transport nodes, merges them together, then returns the processed Place.

```
public function shortestPath($from_nid, $to_nid)
{
        /**Sample:serviceJourneyShortestPath**/
        $cypher = sprintf('MATCH (from:Place),(to:Place), p = shortestPath((from)-[:STOP_ON_
        JOURNEY*..15]-(to)) WHERE id(to) = %s AND id(from) = %s RETURN p', $from_nid, $to_nid);

        $result = $this->client->cypher($cypher);
        $data = $result['results'][0]['data'][0]['row'][0];

        return $data;
}
```

This method is quite important, and actually does the journey planning between two different nodes within the database. It simply takes two node ids as arguments (from and to, respectively) and then uses the shortestPath function to calculate the shortest path between the two. Thanks to the way the nodes are related, they can only ever be connected via a Timetable node, using the STOP_ON_JOURNEY relationship. This means that the only information needed to work out the path is the respective node ids, and that's it. The resulting path between the two nodes is then returned to be used as required by the application.

Routes

This application only has a four different routes, one of which is the homepage (defined in the bootstrap file). The other three routes are used to help with planning journeys, which are explained below:

Journey/Plan

The main route of the application is the one used for planning journeys, and to achieve this it expects two sets of co-ordinates, to and from. Each of these represent the location of the where you'd like to start and end a journey in the form of a longitude and latitude. Rather than going through the full route, the most important parts will be mentioned, starting with getting the nodes required to use the previously mentioned shortestPath method on the journey service.

```
$from_node = $app['journey.service']->closestTransport($from['lat'], $from['lon'], 10.0);
$to_node = $app['journey.service']->closestTransport($to['lat'], $to['lon'], 10.0);
$path = $app['journey.service']->shortestPath($from_node->id, $to_node->id);
```

Using the location data from the supplied to and from nodes, the application is able to find the closest transport node for each location, then with the resulting IDs plan a journey between them. After this stage, we're left with the path between the two nodes, but the path itself isn't too useful so it needs to have some additional processing done on it. The path that is returned works off the following pattern:

```
/* Pattern used:
 *
 * Place node (start location)
 * Relationship between start Place and Timetable
 * Timetable node (used to get the time/transport)
 * Relationship between Timetable and end Place
 * Place node (end location)
 *
 */
```

Provided a successful route can be planned, any stops on the journey will follow this pattern, meaning that the shortest length of a path is 5. The reason behind this is that there is always a start place and an end place, with the timetable node and its relationships in between. This means that if there were an additional Place, the path would be structured as follows:

```
/* Pattern used:
 *
 * Place node
 * Relationship between start Place and Timetable
 * Timetable node
 * Relationship between Timetable and middle Place
 * Place node
 * Relationship between middle Place and Timetable
 * Timetable node
 * Relationship between Timetable and end Place
 * Place node
 *
 */
```

This means that the amount of stops on a journey can be worked out by doing the length of the path -1, divided by four. Knowing this pattern allows for the output to be structured in terms of stopping of the journey, rather than just the raw path, as this may not be too useful. With the path then covered into stops, it's then iterated over once more to get the details of the Timetable node that links the different places together which allows for additional processing to be done based on the properties of said node. Once everything is formatted correctly, the resulting journey is then returned as JSON for use on the front-end of the website.

Journey/Closest

This is a simple route, and simply works out what the closest mode of transport is, based on the location supplied to it. This route then uses the closestTransport method on the Journey service to get the resulting node, which is then returned to the front end of the website.

Journey/Points

Unlike the other routes which are POST, this route is GET, and exists only to supply the front end of the website with all of the different Place nodes, so they can be plotted on a map. To do this, the all method on the Place service is used, and any nodes returned are then processed and returned to the application as JSON.

Each of these routes can be found in JourneyControllerProvider.php (/src/ChrisDKemper/ControllerProvider/JourneyControllerProvider.php) if you'd like to have a look at how they work in more detail. Alternatively, you can search for Sample:JourneyController within the project to find the routes that way.

Commands

To both make things easier and allow for sample data to be loaded into the application, the website has a couple of command line commands it uses to perform certain tasks. These tasks perform different actions, and exist to make the process of performing those actions easier. Rather than going over each line of these files, each command will be explained, and any important functionality or Cypher queries that they do will be mentioned; otherwise all you need to be aware of is that the commands do what they say they do.

Create Indexes

As mentioned earlier, certain indexes are required to allow for spatial queries to take place on Neo4j, and to manage these a small command called IndexCreateCommand (/src/ChrisDKemper/Command/IndexCreateCommand) has been created. This command can be run on the command line by using the following line in Terminal, within the project directory:

```
php bin/console index:create
```

This command takes advantage of some of the methods that were created on the Client, to make creating the required indexes for the site easier. Below are the two main lines from the command, which call the required methods on the client to create the intended index.

```
/**Sample:IndexCreateCommand**/
$spatial_data = $client->createSpatialIndex();
$cypher_index = $client->createCypherIndexForSpatial();
```

The main action within this command comes from calling the "createSpatialIndex" and "createCypherIndexForSpatial" methods on the client as mentioned before. This is just a wrapper to save running these commands manually, but it still exists to allow for the application to be run from an empty database.

Import Bus Stops

Before the application can be of any use, it needs some data. Since everything is built around places, we need to get some of those in first. To do this, a command has been written that imports nodes as "Places" if they don't already exists, and then creates a BusStop node and relates it back to the place. This takes place with the BusStopImportCommand, which also can be run on the command line via the following command which needs to be run in the root directory of the application:

```
php bin/console busstop:import
```

Within the command, the first check that happens is to see whether or not the Place exists within Neo4j or not. A query is done to see if a Place exists with the same name. This is important as you cannot have a BusStop without a Place (as the BusStop relates to the Place) so the place either needs to be fetched (by its name), or created. When the place doesn't exist, the place node is created (with location information) and is then added to the spatial index via the spatialAddNodeToLayer method on the previously included client.

With the Place node either created or fetched, a BusStop node is created and then related to the node. The Cypher code used to relate the two nodes is as follows:

```
/**Sample:BusStopImportCommand**/
MATCH (a:BusStop),(b:Place)
WHERE id(a) = O AND id(b) = 1
CREATE UNIQUE (a)-[r:LOCATED_AT]->(b)
RETURN r
```

This query is adapted from the code, and the 0, and 1 IDs are substituted in for actual IDs in the code, but this example would relate the two nodes, provided that `a` (0) is a BusStop and `b` (1) is a place. When this command runs, it'll go through this process for every BusStop, ensuring it has a Place node to relate to, then creating and relating the nodes as required.

Import Timetables

With the sample bus stations in, it's time to add some timetables. This command works in a similar way to the previous commands in that it creates the required node (Timetable, in this case) and relates it as needed and that's it. The command to import the timetables is called TimetableImportCommand and can be found at /src/ChrisDKemper/Command/TimetableImportCommand.php.

Although this command works similarly to the others, it has a bit more information, as it has both the information for the Timetables, but also for the times for these timetables as well. After the data has been included, the first action to take place is the creation of the Timetable nodes. The timetables have a name, the days of the week the timetable runs on, and the times that the timetable runs on. The timetable is created with this information, and is returned to the command, ready to use.

With the timetable node created, it then needs to be related to the different places it calls at, which it does using the "STOP_ON_JOURNEY" relationship. On this relationship there is also a property of "time" which indicates the amount of time it'll take for the journey to get to that particular "Place". The Cypher used to achieve this can be seen below.

```
/**Sample:TimetableImportCommand**/
MATCH (a:Timetable),(b:Place)
WHERE id(a) = O AND id(b) = 1
CREATE UNIQUE (a)-[r:STOP_ON_JOURNEY {time : 100}]->(b)
RETURN r;
```

This code is run for each of the place nodes on the timetable, with the values for the node ids and time being altered as needed. With the Timetable all linked up to the places it calls it, there now needs to be a Transport node, which is related to the Timetable. This gives the freedom for a Transport to run multiple timetables, and the Cypher used to relate the transport to its timetable can be seen below.

```
MATCH (a:Transport),(b:Timetable)
WHERE id(a) = O AND id(b) = 1
CREATE UNIQUE (a)-[r:RUNS_ON]->(b)
RETURN r;
```

This code then creates the RUNS_ON relationship between the Transport and the Timetable, allowing for the service that runs a particular timetable to be retrieved based on this relationship.

Setting up the Website with Commands

When the website is first provisioned after being downloaded from the github repository, the database will have no nodes in it, so the commands will need to be run in order to seed it with some sample information. As previously mentioned there have been commands created to make these processes easier, so to fill the database with test information, run the following commands in order from the root of the project directory:

```
php bin/console index:create
php bin/console busstop:import
php bin/console timetable:import
```

These are the commands that have been previously covered, and will get the website ready to run. What it looks like

After a lot of set up, it's finally time to see how the website looks, and what it's made up of. Since the purpose of this website is to make journeys, the main view is a full screen map. On the map, there will be a number of different markers on the map, which are the Bus Stops that have been previously imported and will be red. There will also be a blue marker on the screen, which is the "From" marker.

Technology Used

Since this is a Neo4j book, like the construction of the base application, I won't go into too much detail on exactly how everything was put together, but rather will give an overview, and explain any particular bits that are worth mentioning. The map used by the website is Openstreetmap (OSM), which is available by the leaflet.js javascript library. This library makes interacting OSM very easy, and (at least in my opinion) it's very nice to work with. In addition to leaflet, Jquery is used to make some of the interactions on the site a bit easier. There are a number of AJAX requests that are sent by the front end of the website, and Jquery makes that very easy. The only other item worth mentioning is the use of Twitter Bootstrap, which is used for styling the website. The JavaScript and CSS can be found within the web directory of the project, so feel free to have a look in there if you'd like some additional insight into how the website was put together.

How It Works

When the website first loads, the javascript will create a new map using Leaflet. With the map created, using jQuery a GET request will be sent to '/journey/points' to retrieve all of the Places within the system. It then plots each of these onto the map, as well as storing any of the additional properties for the place, to be shown when clicked. If you click on one of the location markers, it'll reveal any information it has about that marker in a sidebar panel, which will appear if it isn't already visible.

The "Form" marker (which can also be dragged around) can also be clicked, which presents two options "Find closest Transport" and "Plan from closest Transport". The first option pretty much does what it says, when the button is clicked; it sends a request to the "/journey/closest" endpoint with the longitude and latitude of the current location. The query is then processed by the controller, and the closest station is returned, which is displayed in the information panel on the page.

Pressing the "Plan from closest Transport" button adds another (draggable) marker to the page, which is used to represent the "To" portion of the journey. If the "From" marker is clicked again, the "Plan from closest Transport" will be replaced with "Set start position to marker" which, when clicked, updates the "From" position within the website. This means that the marker can be moved around and reset, to allow for different journeys to be planned really easily.

Finally, when the "To" marker is clicked, only one option is available, which is "Plan to here". When this option is clicked, a request is sent to "/journey/plan" with the longitude and latitude of the start and end locations of the journey. The resulting journey is then displayed in the information panel of the site.

Using the markers, you can then move them around and plan different journeys very easily.

Summary

This chapter has covered a fair bit of ground, from the installation of the spatial plugin and how to get it functioning, right through to having a website that returned planned journeys. Although this application is written in PHP, it shows what's possible within Neo4j, with very little effort. Since the application code is available at `https://github.com/chrisdkemper/sample-neo4j-php-application`, it's possible to look through the code and see how everything is wired together, to see what you can potentially re-use for your own projects. Although the full application code hasn't been laid out, enough has been shown to illustrate how the site works, whether you're familiar with PHP or not. With that in mind, the Client was created using curl, to give the code as much reusability as possible.

Using the data structure and the Cypher alone, the queries can easily be adapted for your own use. Plus, the application will grow over time, so any new features will be available on github, and if you'd like to find a particular code sample, just search the project for the corresponding comment and any changes made since the book was printed will be explained.

CHAPTER 9

■ ■ ■

Hosting a Neo4j Application

After you've put in the effort to build an application, you'll eventually want to show it to the world, and for that, the application will need to be hosted. There are a huge amount of ways to host content on the internet these days, ranging from static website hosting from GitHub, to shared hosting via a company like site5. Although there are a lot of options out there, that isn't the case when it comes to hosting Neo4j.

To allow for the installation and customization of Neo4j, it means that you can't just go with any old hosting. To get the best results, you either need to go for a dedication Neo4j hosting platform, or install Neo4j yourself on a virtual private server, or VPS. Each of these options has a number of drawbacks and benefits, which we'll go over later, but both are still perfectly viable solutions.

We'll be going over the different options for both, and will also run through an example of hosting Neo4j using the hosting provider Digital Ocean. With that out of the way, let's get straight into it, starting with the technical requirements for Neo4j.

Hosting Requirements

A big thing to keep in mind when hosting your Neo4j application is why you're putting it online in the first place. If you're simply performing some tests on live hardware, you may not need as powerful of a hosting solution as you would for a production environment. The same goes if your application is going to be in production, but isn't going to get much traffic.

Whichever reason you're hosting your application, you should aim to have at least 2GB of RAM dedicated to Neo4j. If you then start performing large amounts of Reads/Writes to the database in too short a time, then it'll start to slow down. If you're just testing, this is manageable, and the usage of the application will no doubt be spiked depending on the usage.

If you're hosting Neo4j for a large amount of intended use, then it's recommended that you have between 8 and 32GB for your hosted solution. This level of use is for applications doing huge amounts of reads/writes every second, if that isn't the case, start out with a 2GB solution and monitor the performance of the hosting. This way, it could be possible to migrate to a better hosting environment, should you need more RAM.

Although RAM is the most important factor, as more RAM makes Neo4j faster, disc space is also important, and should be considered. You need to be sure to try to have at least 10GB of storage available, ideally, through the use of SSDs (solid state drives), which are faster than the disc-based hard drives.

If you're doing a lot of complex queries, it may also be worth checking which processor your hosting provider uses. If possible, it's recommended to have at least an Intel core i3 processor. The processor shouldn't really be an issue, unless you're hosting Neo4j for a high-traffic website or application, and it'll get a lot of use.

Hosting Neo4j

When it comes to making your choice regarding where to host your instance of Neo4j, it comes down to whether or not you want dedicated Neo4j hosting, or if you want to host Neo4j yourself. Each of these solutions has pros and cons associated with it, including sometimes cost. The high-level way to look at it is, if you host Neo4j yourself, you're in complete control, so you can change it as much as desired. This also means you can load your own extensions onto Neo4j to extend its functionality, which isn't always possible with hosted solutions. With dedicated hosting, you're still in control, but must rely on the hosting vendor to have all of the features you need to run your database correctly.

Let's dig into this a bit more, starting with a VPS based solution and then look at some dedicated hosting options.

Choosing a VPS

There are a huge amount of hosting solutions out there now for different use cases. We're going to cover three different solutions: Digital Ocean, Linone, GrapheneDB, and Graphstory. Each are hosting providers in their own right, and have their own benefits and drawbacks, which we'll cover. Enough of that though, let's get straight into things, starting with DigitalOcean.

DigitalOcean

DigitalOcean (DO) has the slogan "Simple Cloud Hosting, Built for Developers" and certainly tries to keep true to that slogan. They've put a lot of work into their product, trying to make it as simple as possible, and you can find them at https://www.digitalocean.com. You can deploy a new SSD cloud server in under 55 seconds according to the website, which is pretty impressive. When you create your cloud server, or Droplet in DO speak, you get the choice of a location, a range of different specifications, and some additional options, including whether or you want private networking. There are a lot of different droplet specifications available, but the more popular configurations can be seen in Figure 9-1.

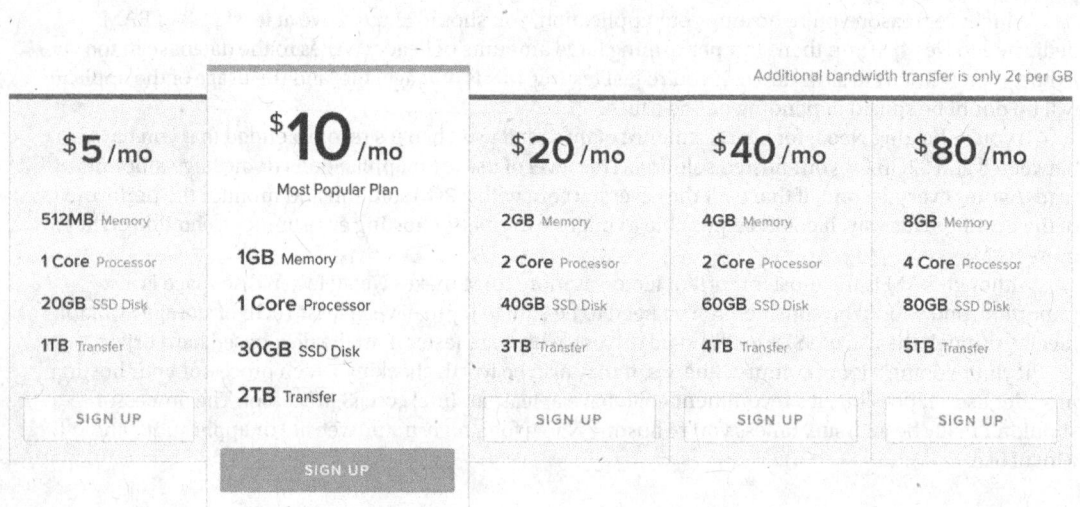

Figure 9-1. The plans available for DigitalOcean droplets

As can be seen by the slider above the prices, rates can also be broken down by hour, rather than a monthly cost. This means if you only need to have a box up for two weeks, then you can calculate the cost for this up front, which is always useful.

The $20/month solution would be enough to host the Neo4j instance and the application using it. This droplet has 2GB of RAM a 2 core processor and 40GB SSD, which is plenty to run Neo4j. Of course, you could still install Neo4j on any of the other droplets, it just wouldn't run as efficiently as it would with more RAM, but since DO has SSDs by default, an increase in speed is gained from that which can offset the RAM requirement. There are also plans above this level for more high traffic applications, topping out with the $640/month which boasts 64GB of RAM, 640GB of storage, and a 20 core CPU, but I think it may be a little excessive for a small Neo4j application.

Features

As you would expect, DO has a decent list of features that help make it what it is. To give a better overview of DO a few will be detailed below, however for a full list of features, be sure to check out the DO website.

Knowledge Base

Although this technically isn't a feature, it's something worth mentioning about DO, as the articles within its knowledge base are brilliant. If you're going to deploy something on DO, or you're having trouble with something on one of your droplets, odds are there's a DO article that can help you. Anyone can get paid to write support articles for DO, so there are a good range of articles, accomplishing a number of different tasks.

High Speed Deployments

We've already covered that you can deploy a droplet in under 55 seconds, which is pretty fast. There's a gif on the homepage of the website which shows how this process works, and how easy it is. You can also save an image of a Droplet and then create new droplets from this image, so you can have pre-built boxes that are ready to go, they just need to be deployed, which is always useful.

Private Networking

Being able to utilize private networking is a big plus, as this allows you to communicate with other droplets you have, but not with the outside world. This means your applications can use internal requests instead of external ones, which is a lot quicker, but also more secure, as any connections made internally, are protected by DOs network.

KVM Virtualization

All of the droplets on DO are virtual, but there's a reason for this. Using virtualized environments means that performance and security are big factors, and are taken very seriously. If any security issues are discovered, they can be addressed a lot easier with virtual environments than physical ones, which is one of the reasons DO is as fast and secure as it is.

Simple Control Panel

DO have spent a lot of time to make their product friendly for developers, and it definitely shows, especially in the control panel. The focus of the control panel is usability, to make it as easy as possible to perform complex actions, and also making sure this process is fast, and easy to understand.

API

Since DO is made for developers, they've also made sure that they not only offer an API, but that it's also as fully featured as possible. The API can be used to accomplish most of the tasks that can be done from the dashboard, including of course, creating Droplets.

99.99% Uptime

When you're hosting anything, you want a guarantee that it's going to be online all the time, and DO does this with a 99.99% uptime SLA. This is achieved by having multiple data centers across the world, and ensuring the communication between these is as fast as possible; in this case, with the use of 10 gig-E networking, to ensure capacity, and redundancy. Each of the datacenters used by DO has battery backups, onsite generators, and physical security, so your droplets not only stay up, they're also secure.

Highlights

If you use DO, you know that you'll have a server that will be up when you need it, and will stay there. Thanks to how easy it is to use, creating new Droplets is easy, and since you only pay for what you use, you can test something out on a droplet, and then destroy it to keep the costs down.

If you use DO a lot, then the API can come in very useful for deploying and destroying your droplets. Since you still get charged if your Droplet is suspended, being able to shut down any unused boxes is always useful. This can of course be achieved in the control panel too, and if you wanted, you could also take an image of the Droplet before it was destroyed, so it can be provisioned again.

One good positive about DO is its smallest droplet, which is $5 a month. Thanks to how cheap it is (provided you don't leave the boxes up after they're needed) it means many can be created at once to test things like clustering configurations, without running up a huge bill.

If you realize you've made one of your droplets too small, and it needs to be upgraded, then no problem. If you power off your Droplet, you can then scale it up as you need to. This means you don't need to provision huge boxes immediately, but you can start smaller and work up.

There may be a time when you pick a promo code for DO that gives you some free credit, but if you've already signed up, you can't use it, right? Not the case, with DO. If you get a promo code, you can redeem it at any time within your profile, which is always a nice to be able to do. Speaking of credit, you can also earn more by referring friends, which again, is a nice thing to be able to do.

Conclusion

DigitalOcean is a brilliant platform, and is more than capable or serving Neo4j, or any other application comfortably. With DOs credit system, keeping on top of your spending is easy, and thanks to its uptime SLA, if you deploy a Droplet, it'll be available 99.99% (until your credit is used up, that is). Whether you're looking to fire up a few servers to test out a cluster, or if you're hosting your production environment, DO can help.

Linode

Another offering in the cloud hosting market is Linode, which offers cloud hosting, with all packages using SSDs. With Linode you get a lot of benefits and features, which we'll cover in a moment, one of which is the ability to deploy a Linde within seconds, at least that's what the website says. Hardware at Linode also runs on a 40GB network, to ensure that any traffic you get, whether internal or external, isn't slowed down by the network. With over 350,000 customers, the people over at https://www.linode.com must be something right, which is evident in their features and their pricing. When deploying a new server (or Linode) you can choose a location within a choice of eight datacenters in three different regions, with a number of packages to choose from, as shown in Figure 9-2.

No Calculator Required

CPU, transfer, storage, and RAM bundled into one simple price.

Linode **1GB**	Linode **2GB**	Linode **4GB**	Linode **8GB**
$**.015**/hr	$**.03**/hr	$**.06**/hr	$**.12**/hr
($10/mo)	($20/mo)	($40/mo)	($80/mo)
1 GB RAM	2 GB RAM	4 GB RAM	8 GB RAM
1 CPU Core	2 CPU Cores	4 CPU Cores	6 CPU Cores
24 GB SSD Storage	48 GB SSD Storage	96 GB SSD Storage	192 GB SSD Storage
2 TB Transfer	3 TB Transfer	4 TB Transfer	8 TB Transfer
40 Gbit Network In	40 Gbit Network In	40 Gbit Network In	40 Gbit Network In
125 Mbit Network Out	250 Mbit Network Out	500 Mbit Network Out	1000 Mbit Network Out
Sign Up	Sign Up	Sign Up	Sign Up

Figure 9-2. *The price of the different Linodes at* https://www.linode.com

The prices are broken down into hourly and monthly costs, which gives a good overview of what your particular Linode will cost, especially if you're going to have it up for less than a month. Each Linode is actually billed by the hourly rate, with a cap set to the monthly cost, so you're never going to be overpaying here, unless you go over your usage cap, that is.

For hosting Neo4j, the Linode 2GB package would be sufficient to host both Neo4j, and also the application that's using it without any real issue. Although having more RAM is always beneficially, the SSD hosting used helps compensate for this, so with 2GB of RAM and SSDs, a small-scale Neo4j database should be perfectly fine. You can also go all the way up to a Linode 96GB plan, which sports 96GB of RAM, 20 CPU cores, 1920GB storage, and a $1.44 / hour ($960 / month) price tag. This is of course an instance for a huge application, and most likely overkill for a number of applications, but it's nice to know the option is there either way.

Features

To compete in the hosting market, your features need to do the talking, and Linode certainly talks a lot with all of the features it has to offer. We'll go through a few noteworthy ones in a moment, but for a full list of features, check out the website.

Intel E5 Processors

Linode doesn't just have any processors; they have Intel E5 Processors. These are high-end, server-based CPUs, and they're pretty fast. This is good to know if your application happens to do any CPU-intensive actions. Even if this isn't the case for your application, it'll still run smoother and faster thanks to these chips, so it's definitely a good benefit to Linode.

Nodebalancers

An available feature with Linode is the use of a Nodebalancer, which is a load balancer, but with a bit of a difference from others. On a base level, what the Nodebalancer does is sit in front of your backend Linodes and takes large amounts of traffic. Any requests are then passed off to the required backend Linodes, but there's a little more to it that than. It'll also monitor each backend Linode, and if for whatever reason it's in an unhealthy state, the request won't be routed to it.

The best thing about the Nodebalancers is how easy they are to use. They can be added at any time, and at $20.00/month, adding one Nodebalancer could replace the need for an additional server instance, thanks to how it shares traffic. Although you may not always need them, it's always good to know a feature like this is available, and is easy to use.

Longview

Monitoring your servers is always a good thing, and Longview makes this as easy for you as possible. To make managing multiple Linodes easier, Longview lets you check the status of all your servers on one page, rather than having to manage them individually. With the free tier, you get the last 12 hours of data, with updates every 5 minutes. You can also upgrade to pro for $20.00/month for the 1–3 systems, with larger packages available for larger setups. With pro, you get all of your historical data and updates every 60 seconds. This essentially means, if you have an outage over the weekend, you can look back on Monday to see what happened and try to fix the issue.

Managed

Sometimes you just don't want to spend the time maintaining a server to ensure it's always running. Linode knows this, and they also offer a managed package, which means once the application is running, they'll keep it running. If you commit to at least 3 months, Linode will even help with the migration from your existing hosting to a managed Linode. At $100.00/mo, this isn't a cheap service but if you're in a position where downtime isn't an option for your application, it's nice to know Linode can have your back.

StackScripts

One common thing when provisioning servers, is that there can be a lot of repetition, so you'll end up doing the same steps a number of times on multiple servers, which can get annoying. Other people have had these thoughts and written ways to automate these things, and thanks to StackScripts, they can be yours to use. There are a number of different environments that can be provisioned through answering a couple of questions required for the installation and then setting it away. Essentially, it's always worth checking the StackScripts library to see if what you're about to do has been added as a StackScript, so it can be run with minimal effort.

Professional Services

Through its various services, Linode offers a lot of different features, and if you only want a website migration, Linode can quote for that. If you aren't sure on the exact server configuration needs, or need some help streamlining a server, these are things Linode can help with. Each service is done on a quote basis, so you won't know how much something will cost beforehand, but it's an option that's there, if required.

Conclusion

Linode is brilliant hosting platform, and can be the home for both small and large applications. Thanks to its hour-based billing, you know how much you'll be paying a month, which saves being worried about whether or not you'll overpay. Of course, if you use all of your bandwidth and need some more, there will be a charge for that, but if it's happening consistently, you can upgrade.

Speaking of upgrading, this process is made as simple as possible in Linode, and if you need to upgrade an instance, just go to its control panel, make the needed change, and let Linode do the rest. If you realize you're spending too much time monitoring your services because they've grown above your control, why not get Linode in to help? With its reasonable prices and free offerings, it can be a stable platform for any application as it starts with features to support it as it grows.

Linode also has a referral scheme, whereby you can earn additional Linode credit to help your servers stay up even longer, and also share the love you have for Linode, of course.

■ **Note** Of course you can manage the installation of Neo4j yourself, but that isn't the only way to do things. As with other database systems, there are companies that offer remote Neo4j hosting. This means you can have your database and your application in two separate places. There can be a slight delay thanks to it being remote, but that sacrifice is worth it, so that you know your database is going to be there, even if your application isn't.

GrapheneDB

One of the offerings in the Neo4j hosting market is GrapheneDB, and hosting Neo4j is what they do. It offers a lot of the features you'd want in Neo4j hosting, as well as still giving you full access to your data. GrapheneDB hosts your database on one of two systems, AWS (Amazon Web Services) or Microsoft Azure. Both systems are cloud-based hosting platforms that are more than capable of hosting your database. It's also possible to use GrapheneDB as a Heroku extension, which gives even more flexibility to the service.

GrapheneDB takes the pain of doing the deployment on these services yourself, and instead gives an easy to use the website, with a number of top-quality features. When your server is provisioned on GrapheneDB, it is then available to communicate with via REST. To make this even easier, GrapheneDB also included a number of "Getting started" snippets for many popular programming languages.

There are free plans available on both platforms, but these aren't intended to be used in production environments, but rather for hobby use only. The plans for use on AWS can be seen in Figure 9-3, as it has an additional plan, and with the first package in each being the same price, AWS made sense. On the GrapheneDB website (http://www.graphenedb.com) you can see a full list of plans and features, but we'll just run through a notable few for now, just remember to check the website if you'd like additional information.

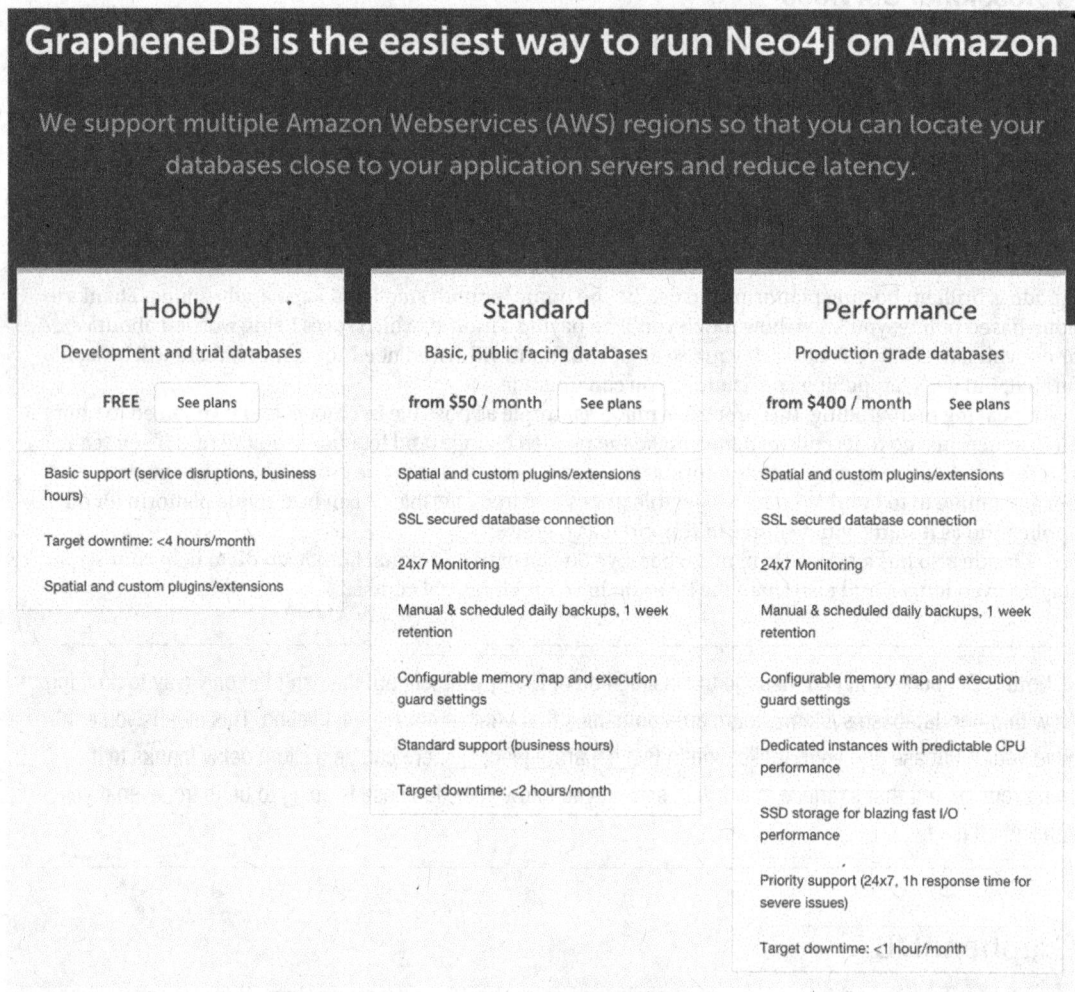

Figure 9-3. *The pricing structure for hosting Neo4j on AWS, using GrapheneDB*

The first thing to note is the price of the first package, which is the one intended for personal use. You really don't get a lot with the free package, and it's capped at 1K nodes and 10K nodes. You can increase this to 100k nodes and 1M relationships, for $9/mo. Although you don't get a lot of space for storage, you do get a hosted Neo4j instance that can be used for testing. That being said, it will be unpredictable on performance and may not always be available, but for testing that's just fine.

From $50/month you get into the standard packages, which have a lot more features, including SSL, backups, access to custom Neo4j settings, and more. The interesting thing about the $50 plan is the hardware, which is 512MB of RAM and 1G storage. This plan is still classed as Standard, so if you're running an average-sized website you should be fine on this plan.

When it comes to hosting a large database, you'll want the Professional plan, which starts from $400/mo where you get 3GB of RAM and 40GB of storage. You get dedicated servers here, so you know the performance you're getting is going to be consistent, as well as everything else from the previous packages. You also get a target downtown of less than 1 hour a month.

Features

In the paid packages there are a number of features, so let's go into them in a bit more detail, shall we?

24/7 Monitoring

If your usage or nodes spike for some reason, you'll be notified but engineers will ensure your database is running, 24/7. Of course, depending on your plan, there will be some downtime over the month, but outside of these scheduled occasions, any malicious or unscheduled outage will be resolved.

Cloud Scaling

Thanks to the databased being hosted on cloud hosting platforms, it allows for great scalability. It'll be able to handle the traffic being thrown at it without falling over, and upgrading couldn't be easier. If you need more out of your database, you can upgrade just as easily as you signed up, then let the website do the work.

Support

When subscribed to a Standard or Performance plan, you then get access to the expert support team at GrapheneDB. This isn't just support with issues or bugs; this is support for you as a developer, and the team can help with anything from query optimization to driver configuration. With this support, your application and database will be running as smoothly as it possibly can.

Backups

Having a backup system in place is always important, and here is no exception. Your hosted database will be backed up on a daily basis. You can also manually initiate snapshots of the database, so you can always backup before that big migration. The daily backups will be kept a total of 7 days, but can be downloaded at any time, so if you like, you can download a backup manually each week. You can also restore from a backup at any time, so if the worst does happen and data is lost, or you need to revert back for whatever reason, the option is there.

Operational Dashboard

Being able to see how your database is running is important, so on your dashboard, it's possible to see streaming download of Neo4js server logs. This gives the flexibility to quickly get a handle on what's happening within the database without manually looking at the logs. So if your website is running slow for some reason, you can check for issues.

At the Performance tier, you also get access to detailed server metrics for your dedicated database instance. In addition to knowing how the database is running, you can also make sure the server is running.

Extensible

One of the issues with hosted solutions can be the inability to customize the hosted instance, but that isn't the case this time. You enable popular Neo4j extensions, as well as being able to code your own. This allows you to customize your database to your hearts content, as it should be.

Conclusion

GrapheneDB has a brilliant set of features and is very easy to use. It takes no time at all to sign up and create a sandbox database, which is ready to be used in your development project, without any mess. The inclusion of the quick start code samples to communicate over REST is brilliant, and really speeds things up.

When your data is the most important thing, having it looked after and backed up is what you always want to do, so knowing GrapheneDB takes care of all that is a big relief. In some instances, the price point may be a factor, but for that price you get access to a lot of features, including access to the expert support team. As well as knowing your database will be kept online, you also have the ability to still extend and customize it, so your database can grow with you. Overall it's a brilliant service, even just for the free tier alone, and the ability to integrate that into Heroku gives some brilliant development power, which is always a good thing.

Graphstory

Another space in the Neo4j hosting market is Graphstory. Although there is a free tier available, and a number of smaller ones too, the main action here is in the production-based bundles. It's possible to get signed up for a free account very quickly, and you're given instant access to a database. This database is functioning and available via REST, but its storage capabilities or limitations are unknown.

There is a developer plan, which gives you access to 1GB of RAM, 5GB of SDD storage and on-demand backups for $9.99/mo. Above this plan, there are also Startup (from $49.99/mo) plans, Premium (from $299.99) plans, and the Enterprise plan, which requires you to contact them for a price. Although the pricing of these plans seems expensive, you do get a lot for you money, at least with the Premium plan.

The Startup plan is a more equipped version of the developer plan, offering 2GB RAM, 40GB SSD, and a 2 core CPU machine. If you upgrade your starter plan to the S3 package at $149.99/mo, you then get access to the main weapon of Graphstory, its clustering. In Figure 9-4, you can see the options that come with the Premium level cluster services, and the price associated with them. At the standard level tier, the staging machine is 2GB instead of 4GB, but this can be increased by jumping to the $199.99/month plan.

	PREMIUM - P1	PREMIUM - P2	PREMIUM - P3	PREMIUM - P4
Staging Servers	1	2	2	2
Processor	2 Cores	2 Cores	2 Cores	4 Cores
Memory	2 GB	4 GB	4 GB	8 GB
Storage	40 GB	60 GB	60 GB	60 GB
Transfer	3 TB	4 TB	5 TB	6 TB
Production Servers	2	3	3	5
Processor	2 Cores	4 Cores	8 Cores	8 Cores
Memory	4 GB	8 GB	16 GB	16 GB
Storage	60 GB	80 GB	80 GB	160 GB
Transfer	6 TB	8 TB	10 TB	12 TB
Backups	Twice Daily	Once Hourly	Twice Hourly	Twice Hourly + Offsite
Support	Email (24 X 7)	Email (24 X 7)	Phone & Email (24 X 7)	Dedicated Support Contact
Price (per month)	$299.99	$799.99	$1999.99	$2999.99
	SIGN UP	SIGN UP	SIGN UP	SIGN UP

Figure 9-4. *The premium plans available to Graphstory customers.*

As you can see, the options for clusters are crazy, and that's all taken care of for you, without having to worry about it. Sure, it's a lot of money, but you also get a fully maintained cluster that isn't going to fall down, no matter what happens. With the highest tier, you also get twice hourly backups that are also offsite, so when it comes to keeping data safe, they aren't playing around.

Conclusion

Graphstory looks to be a very powerful provider when it comes to hosting. They even utilize DigitalOcean for hosting the servers. Although it has a lot of features, it's really geared towards larger applications, rather than just a regular developer. The features offered aren't detailed too heavily on the website, because they want you to get in touch and ask. This is fine and the platform itself seems very solid, however for developers building smaller applications, it may not be the best solution.

A Hosting Example

The best way to go through hosting Neo4j, is to host Neo4j. To show this, I'll be running through the process used to host the Pokémon app (which was used to gather the data used in Chapter 7) which is a PHP-based application, backed by Neo4j.

Hosting on DigitalOcean

In this case, my choice of hosting provider was DigitalOcean, primarily because I had credit in my account that I could use. Also, I find DigitalOcean very easy to use so it just made sense to host it there. Other than having the credit, in terms of cost and features, there could have been other choices used to host the application (Linode, for one) but this application isn't going to be hosted long term, so DigitalOcean made sense.

Since installation instructions are one of the things that have a habit of changing, the commands used here will be stored in a GitHub gist, so any changes can be documented there because books cannot be corrected after print. The URL for the gist is GIST_URL_HERE, but if you check my gists (ChrisDKemper) you should find it there.

Creating a Droplet

To start things off, a droplet needs to be created so I actually have something to deploy Neo4j to. Since I had the credit available, I decided to go with the $20/month instance which gives me 40GB of storage, and 2GB of RAM, more than enough to run a small PHP application and Neo4j. I also opted for a London-based droplet, as this is closer to me, which can been seen along with the rest of the setup in Figure 9-5.

Figure 9-5. *The setup used to create the Pokémon droplet*

I added my MacBook's SSH key to the box to give me access to it, then set things away and within a minute, I had my running droplet.

Install Neo4j

Using Terminal, it was time to SSH into the droplet and get ready to install Neo4j. Since this droplet is running Ubuntu, it's possible to use the information from Chapter 3 to our advantage here, as an Ubuntu server was used there. It's worth noting that I've SSH'd into the droplet as `root`, so all of the commands are run as `root` which essentially means every command has a `sudo` infant of it, and `root` saves you from doing that. First, we first need to add the Neo4j key to `aptitute`, to give it access to the code repositories, once they're added. To add the key, the following command is used:

```
wget -O - http://debian.neo4j.org/neotechnology.gpg.key | apt-key add -
```

The key will be fetched from the Neo4j website, and added to `apt` and when it's done, you should see OK, with your prompt back to normal. With access now granted to the repository, it's now time to actually add the Neo4j repository so it can be found, which is done like so:

```
echo 'deb http://debian.neo4j.org/repo stable/' > /etc/apt/sources.list.d/neo4j.list
```

There won't be any interaction from the Terminal here. It'll just run and you'll be presented back with the terminal prompt. The next stage is to perform an update, and by doing so, pull in the new definitions, which will allow Neo4j to be installed. To run the update, use the following code:

```
apt-get update -y
```

With everything up to date, it's time to actually install Neo4j. Rather than opting to say `Yes` to every installation, I used the -y flag, so the install just runs, and installs everything. The command looks like so:

```
apt-get install neo4j -y
```

After many output lines from the installation, you'll be prompted saying Neo4j is up and running at localhost:7474, and you may also see a warning regarding the number of max open files, which will look something like this:

■ **Warning**   Max 1024 open files allowed, minimum of 40,000 recommended. See the Neo4j manual.

To solve this problem, we need to increase the max open files. It is possible to do this using the `ulimit` command, but that's only for the active session, and this needs to be all the time. The first file that needs amending is `/etc/security/limits.conf` which needs the following lines added to it:

```
root    soft    nofile  40000
root    hard    nofile  40000
```

These lines give the root user permission to have this many files open at once. The next step is to allow this property to be read, by editing another file, `/etc/pam.d/su`, and uncommenting, or adding, the following line:

```
session    required    pam_limits.so
```

This means that from now on, every session with the user, that user will be allowed to have 40,000 open files, which is what we want. For this to take effect, the server needs to be restarted, which is done by using the following command:

```
sudo shutdown -r now
```

Using this command will kill any connections you have to the server so don't worry about that, just wait a little while for it to reboot and SSH back in. With the code in place, Neo4j will now run without displaying the error, which is good news. Although Neo4j is running, if you tried to go to IP_address:7474, you wouldn't see anything. This is because by default Neo4j only serves to localhost, which isn't what we want. This is easily fixed though, and it involves changing a file, which is located at `/etc/neo4j/neo4j-server.properties`
In the file, you'll want to locate the following line:

```
org.neo4j.server.webserver.address=0.0.0.0
```

This will need to be uncommented, and then `0.0.0.0` needs to be changed to the IP address of the Droplet. With that change made, it's just a case of restarting Neo4j once again to get everything working.

```
service neo4j-service restart
```

The browser is now available at IP:7474, which means an important thing can now happen: setting the password for your database, as using default values in production is a bad idea. Also, because Neo4j also thinks this is important you need to change the password before it'll work, so it's better to make it something secure now.

Some Other Dependencies

Before the Pokémon website can run, it needs a few other things, such as PHP, Nginx, Git (for the cloning of the repository), and a couple of other things. The installation of these things isn't really relevant to the hosting of Neo4j, so I won't go into detail.

An Annoying Warning

When starting the Neo4j service, you may see the following warning:

■ **Warning**   not changing user

This warning isn't something to be worried about, as it's not actually true anyway. Neo4j needs to be run as `root`, but does actually switch users, and the process itself, runs as the `neo4j` user. At the time of writing, I couldn't find a reason or solution for this warning, as Neo4j is actually running just fine. It seems worth mentioning, as it seems like it could be quite an important warning, but in fact, it just lies.
Of course, things do change, so if a solution or reason has been found since the book was published, it'll be inside available on the GitHub gist mentioned earlier, which will contain the full installation instructions for Neo4j, kept up to date with changes, so if the command in the book doesn't work, check the Gist.

Using a Standalone Neo4j Server

From the previous research on hosted Neo4j solutions, it seems you can easily run Neo4j on environments that have specs which are a lot less than the minimum specs required. With that in mind, it makes sense to put Neo4j on its own server (or droplet, in this case) which will mean I can dedicate all of the available resources to Neo4j, and it won't have to share with the application instance. Both servers in this case would be the $5/pm droplet, which even though it has two servers, it's half the running cost of the larger one.

In reality, nothing much needs to change here. The previous installation steps can be followed to install Neo4j, but instead of installing the rest of the application on the same server, it's installed on a different one. In this particular case, private networking is required for both of these boxes, as the application will communicate with Neo4j via the internal IP address, not the external one. Earlier we set the org.neo4j.server. webserver.address property in the /etc/neo4j/neo4j-server.properties file, which now needs to be set to the internal IP of the Neo4j droplet. This ensures that no external traffic can access the Neo4j instance, and it can only be reached from inside the Digital Ocean network. In terms of private networking, you need to ensure any droplets you'd like to communicate with each other are in the same datacenter, so with this in mind, both the droplets I'm using are in the London datacenter.

The final step is to change the main application to use the internal IP address of the Neo4j droplet, rather than `localhost` like it had done previously, since everything was hosted on the same machine. There will be a decrease in speed because the database is now on another server, but since Digital Ocean's internal network is around 1GB/ps, and the application utilizes a queue system, any reduction in speed won't be noticed by the user. This essentially means the hosting costs are halved, and the app remains the same speed, with Neo4j getting more dedicated resources since it no longer has to share, which is a win/win/win.

Using ansible to Deploy Automatically

Although there isn't another Neo4j instance needed for the Pokémon application, there will be other times that one is, and for that reason it's good to look at automated deployments. Of course, you could easily manually set up Neo4j on a new server using the previously mentioned commands, and that'd be fine, but wouldn't it be nicer to just hit a button and have all that work done for you? I thought that, so I ended up looking at Ansible.

In Ansible 2.0 (currently in beta, at the time of writing) it has Digital Ocean integration. This is currently available but the 2.0 version uses V2 of the Digital Ocean API, and since I like Digital Ocean, I figured I'd go with it. With that out of the way, below is a code sample that includes two Ansible files, the playbook, and the variables (vars.yml) file.

```
##vars.yml

#DigitalOcean stuff
digital_ocean_token: TOKEN_HERE
digital_ocean_ssh_name: ocelot.pub
digital_ocean_ssh_pub: "{{ lookup('file', '/vagrant/ansible/ssh/ocelot.pub') }}"
digital_ocean_ssh_key: /vagrant/ansible/ssh/ocelot
digital_ocean_droplet_name: ocelotdroplet
digital_ocean_droplet_size_id: 512mb
digital_ocean_droplet_region_id: lon1
digital_ocean_droplet_image_id: 13089493
digital_ocean_droplet_private_networking: yes
#Neo4j stuff
neo4j_config_file: "{{ lookup('file', '/vagrant/ansible/neo4j/neo4j-server.properties') }}"
```

```yaml
##neo4j.yml
---
- hosts: 127.0.0.1
  connection: local
  vars_files:
    - vars.yml
  tasks:
    - name: Ensure ocelot key is available
      digital_ocean:
        state=present
        command=ssh
        name="ocelot.pub"
        ssh_pub_key="{{ digital_ocean_ssh_pub }}"
        api_token="{{ digital_ocean_token }}"
      register: ssh_key
    - name: Create a digital ocean droplet
      digital_ocean:
        state=present
        command=droplet
name="{{ digital_ocean_droplet_name }}"
        size_id="{{ digital_ocean_droplet_size_id }}"
        region_id="{{ digital_ocean_droplet_region_id }}"
        image_id="{{ digital_ocean_droplet_image_id }}"
        wait_timeout=500
        private_networking={{ digital_ocean_droplet_private_networking }}
        ssh_key_ids={{ ssh_key.ssh_key.id }}
        api_token="{{ digital_ocean_token }}"
        unique_name=yes
      register: my_droplet
    - name: Register droplet as dynamic host
      add_host:
        name="{{ digital_ocean_droplet_name }}"
        groups=droplets
        ansible_ssh_host="{{ my_droplet.droplet.networks.v4[1].ip_address }}"
        ansible_ssh_user=root
        ansible_ssh_private_key_file="{{ digital_ocean_ssh_key }}"
- hosts: droplets
  tasks:
  - debug: msg="{{ ansible_eth0.ipv4.address }}"
  - debug: msg="{{ ansible_eth1.ipv4.address }}"
  - name: Check if neo4j is installed
    command: dpkg --get-selections | grep neo4j
    register: neo4j_check
  - name: Key1
    shell: wget -O - http://debian.neo4j.org/neotechnology.gpg.key | apt-key add -
    when: neo4j_check.stdout == ""
  - name: Key2
    shell: echo 'deb http://debian.neo4j.org/repo stable/' > /etc/apt/sources.list.d/neo4j.
list
    when: neo4j_check.stdout == ""
  - name: Install Neo4j
```

```
    apt: name=neo4j update_cache=yes state=latest
    when: neo4j_check.stdout == ""
- name: Set the correct address
  lineinfile: dest=/etc/neo4j/neo4j-server.properties
  regexp=^#org.neo4j.server.webserver.address=
  line=org.neo4j.server.webserver.address={{ ansible_eth1.ipv4.address }}
  when: neo4j_check.stdout == ""
  notify:
     - restart neo4j
handlers:
- name: restart neo4j
  service: name=neo4j-service state=restarted
- name: restart machine
command: shutdown -r now "Ansible updates triggered"
async: 0
poll: 0
ignore_errors: true
- name: waiting for server to come back
local_action: wait_for host={{ inventory_hostname }}
              state=started
sudo: false
```

This file would need to be need to be split up, and is adapted from a project called Ocelot which I'm working on. It'll work independent of it of course, it's just the names and paths that are used really, but those can be easily changed. With a couple of changes, the playbook can be created for different applications or for droplets with different names for multiple Neo4j instances. Automated deployments always have some benefit, even if that benefit is ease of use. You may of course still need to do some manual changes to these environments when they're created, but it will save time in the long run. The code used here will be available as a gist (https://gist.github.com/chrisdkemper/7a9fff23309c7cf55963) so any updates will be available there.

To make this process a little easier, I created a small website to make running these playbooks easier. The project is currently very young, but can be found at https://github.com/chrisdkemper/ocelot and will no doubt change and improve, but it's called Ocelot, and it allows you to run a playbook and watch the terminal output in the browser. It's also on Vagrant so it'll run on any system capable of running it, so hopefully it'll be of use to somebody. Anyway, enough about that. If the Playbook will be useful to you then by all means use it, it'll be kept up to date on the gist, so even after this book is printed, the gist will always be correct.

Optimizing Neo4j

When it comes to optimizing Neo4j there are a couple of different approaches. There are small changes that can help, but could be left as defaults, such as optional extras. The other side is the more complex side, which includes configuring the server in a certain way, tweaking the JVM settings, and so on. We'll be covering the former side of the optimizations, as these changes can make things a little more secure, with a small amount of effort.

To make things easier each one will be broken down into its command. First, we have a couple of additions to the neo4j-server.properties file, which is located at /etc/neo4j/neo4j.properties on a default installation. The following line adds a max timeout to a query, to save on runaway queries that traverse the graph multiple times. Any queries will be rolled back because they're in a transaction, so no damage will be done.

```
org.neo4j.server.transaction.timeout=60
```

Next is changing the org.neo4j.server.manage.console_engines property to match the following. This disables the use of the consoles available in webadmin, so no malicious actions can happen. You should be safe, but it's a good failsafe unless you use the shell commands; in which case leave the line as it is. For no console, mirror the next line.

```
org.neo4j.server.manage.console_engines=
```

Each of the following lines need to be done in a neo4j.properties file which will need to be created in the same directory as the neo4j-server.properties file.

```
execution_guard_enabled=true
```

This teamed with the previous line in the neo4j-server.properties stops queries that would otherwise potentially run forever, which is a good failsafe for production servers.

```
dbms.pagecache.memory=128m
```

The final change is setting a pagecache. This doesn't need to be too much, in this case it's 128MB, but if you don't have much memory available, as long as this value is around 2MB (it can't be 0) you'll be fine.

To keep these valid, these config values will be available in a gist () so if there's any updates, they'll be logged there. This gist and the others from the book will be available at `https://gist.github.com/chrisdkemper`.

Summary

This chapter has given a lot of information on how to host Neo4j. There are choices for giving it a try, hosting small instances, right up to automated deployments. Since the instructions are there (and available in a gist if they change) the instructions to set up Neo4j on any Linux server and you'll be ready to go. For local testing a server, it's also possible to use the vagrant box I set up, which is available at `https://github.com/chrisdkemper/neo4j-vagrant`, just in case you need it.

The optimization gist will be kept up to date as time goes on, by anyone that contributes to it, so if you keep checking back it'll be a useful resource when it comes to optimizing a server. Then you'll be ready to have your own hosted Neo4j application for whatever you need it for, even if it's just for testing.

If you're up for automating your deployments, then the Ansible playbook will come in useful to deploy Neo4j instances even easier. Also if you want it even easier, there's always the Ocelot project, which can found at `https://github.com/chrisdkemper/ocelot`.

Hopefully the book has given you a good journey into Neo4j, showing you enough about Cypher to get started and even how to do recommendations. It will be enough to start any project (hopefully) with enough reference to give the extra information needed for those more challenging queries. If you like the book, please get in touch on Twitter (@chriskemper, drop me an e-mail, or just get in touch some how. I'd love to hear feedback, good or bad.

Index

Get the eBook for only $5!

Why limit yourself?

Now you can take the weightless companion with you wherever you go and access your content on your PC, phone, tablet, or reader.

Since you've purchased this print book, we're happy to offer you the eBook in all 3 formats for just $5.

Convenient and fully searchable, the PDF version enables you to easily find and copy code—or perform examples by quickly toggling between instructions and applications. The MOBI format is ideal for your Kindle, while the ePUB can be utilized on a variety of mobile devices.

To learn more, go to www.apress.com/companion or contact support@apress.com.

Printed in the United States
By Bookmasters